GĪTĀR GĀN

Singing the Song Divine

By His Divine Grace
A.C. Bhaktivedanta Swami Prabhupāda
Translated by Kalakaṇṭha Dāsa & Swarūpa Krishna Dāsa

Gītār Gān - Singing the Song Divine

Kalakaṇṭha Dāsa
carlwoodham@gmail.com

Published by Sweetsong Books
ISBN: 979-8-9873335-0-1

Design & Layout by:
HoofprintMedia.com

Gītār Gān

Singing the Song Divine

By His Divine Grace

A.C. Bhaktivedanta Swami Prabhupāda

Translated by Kalakaṇṭha Dāsa & Swarūpa Krishna Dāsa

Table of Contents

Foreword	7
Introduction	10
Chapter 1: The Yoga of Suffering and Distress	13
Chapter 2: Knowledge of the Soul and Body by Analytical Study	21
Chapter 3: Discharge of One's Prescribed Duty of Devotional Service to the Supreme Lord	37
Chapter 4: Transcendental Knowledge	47
Chapter 5: Action in Kṛṣṇa Consciousness	57
Chapter 6: Practice in the State of Transcendence	65
Chapter 7: Knowledge of the Absolute	75
Chapter 8: Attaining the Supreme	83
Chapter 9: The Most Confidential Knowledge	89
Chapter 10: The Opulence of the Absolute	97
Chapter 11: The Universal Form	105
Chapter 12: Devotional Service	121
Chapter 13: Nature, the Enjoyer and Consciousness	127
Chapter 14: The Three Modes of Material Nature	135
Chapter 15: The Yoga of the Supreme Person	141
Chapter 16: The Divine and Demonic Natures	147
Chapter 17: The Divisions of Faith	153
Chapter 18: Conclusion: The Perfection of Renunciation	159
Conclusion	172
About the Complete Edition	173
About the Authors	186
Acknowledgments	188
Endnotes	189

Foreword

I was the type of annoying child who constantly asks questions. "Why do I have to make my bed if I am just going to go back into it tonight? Why do I have to eat everything on my plate? Why do I have to be nice to that lady I don't like?"

This tendency to question everything increased as I grew to be a teenager in the rebellious 1960's. "Why can't we have peace? What is the purpose of life? Why do bad things happen to good people? Why is one person born rich and another born poor?"

Seeking answers, I scoured the standard books for seekers: *I Ching, Autobiography of a Yogi, The Tibetan Book of the Dead, Dharma Bums, The Way of Zen, Siddhartha, The Doors of Perception, The Teachings of Don Juan,* etc. After all that reading, however, I still had many unanswered questions, for none of these books had significantly changed or improved my life.

One day while scanning the metaphysical books in a friend's home library, I came across the *Bhagavad-gītā*. The book seemed to jump off the shelf into my hand. What I found in those pages overwhelmed me with a wealth of knowledge that answered all the big questions and began to radically transform my life in a most wonderful way. Later I met devotees of Krishna who showed me further how to apply the wisdom of the *Gītā* in every aspect of life. All this happened over fifty years ago and yet the *Bhagavad-gītā* still directs and enriches my life. It is a book that just keeps on giving.

My story is not unique. Thousands of lives have been changed by contact with the *Bhagavad-gītā*, the essence of all the teachings of the Vedic literatures. In India, great teachers and spiritual luminaries from all schools of philosophy have all drunk the nectar of *Bhagavad-gītā* and drawn inspiration from the spring of that eternal wisdom. In the West also, the *Bhagavad-gītā* guided and inspired great thinkers such as Albert Einstein, Leo Tolstoy, Henry David Thoreau, Ralph Waldo Emerson, T.S. Elliot, and Carl Jung, as well as modern day celebrities such as George Harrison, Will Smith and Jim Carrey. All have had life-changing encounters with this sacred text.

The *Bhagavad-gītā*'s message—the Supreme Being guiding an individual soul trapped and groping in darkness on the battlefield of worldly life—indeed relates in all times to all people. According to Aldous Huxley, "The *Bhagavad-Gītā* is the most systematic statement of spiritual evolution of endowing value to mankind. It is one of the most clear and comprehensive summaries of perennial philosophy ever revealed; hence its enduring value is relevant not only to India but to all of humanity."

It was the life mission of my spiritual teacher, Śrīla A.C. Bhaktivedanta Swami Prabhupāda, known as Śrīla Prabhupāda, to share the ancient spiritual wisdom of the *Bhagavad-gītā*. His English translation "*Bhagavad-gītā As It Is*," with elaborate explanations for each verse, is the most widely read *Gītā* ever published. He also creatively engaged art, music, drama, dioramas, poetry, and even vegetarian food to make the message of *Bhagavad-gītā* understandable and attractive to everyone.

One of Śrīla Prabhupāda's creative approaches was his writing of *Gītār Gān*, a beautiful and easily understood poetic rendition of the *Bhagavad-gītā*, aimed at making its wisdom more accessible to Bengali-speaking people. His strategy was a grand success, as the Bengali populace loved it. One distributor reported that bookstore owners said they had never seen a book sell so well. "When displayed in Bengali villages," he said, "people crowd around to buy it and carefully wrap their copies in cloth to take back home. Everywhere I go people ask, 'Where is *Gītār Gān*?' They love the poetry because it is so easy to chant or sing."
In this same creative spirit, Kalakaṇṭha Das has found new ways to bring the Vedic wisdom to Western audiences, including various English poetic translations of Sanskrit books that have been widely appreciated. In this, his latest effort, he and Svarūpa Krishna Das present the first full English version of *Gītār Gān*.

Kalakaṇṭha Das is a gifted poet who has, remarkably, created a captivating, rhythmic flow of rhymes while maintaining the integrity of a deeply philosophical text. By examining the Bengali/English synonyms in the work of Svarūpa Krishna Das, it is easy to see how faithful Kalakaṇṭha Das has been to Śrīla Prabhupāda's original. Kalakaṇṭha Das also helps the newcomer navigate the text with useful footnotes.

Both veterans and newcomers to *Bhagavad-gītā* will appreciate this highly readable and inspiring book. Rarely does one find answers to the big questions in such an enjoyable way.

Sitala Devi, ACBSP
Author, *The Glorious Life of Śrīla Narottama Dasa Thakur*

Introduction

In 1962, working alone with a manual typewriter, Śrīla Prabhupāda took time off from his translation of the massive *Śrimad-Bhāgavatam* to condense the *Bhagavad-gītā's* seven hundred verses into simple rhyming Bengali couplets. This book, called *Gītār Gān*, was first published in full in 1973 and is still widely popular throughout Bengal and Bangladesh. The book in your hands presents *Gītār Gān* fully translated in English for the first time.

Of the world's sixty-five hundred languages, the melodic Bengali language is the sixth most widely spoken. Bengali speakers have savored the profound teachings of *Bhagavad-gītā* through Śrīla Prabhupāda's simple *Gītār Gān*. Our translation aims to do the same for English speakers.

Our late friend Bhakti Caru Swami set the Bengali verses of *Gītār-gān* to music and published its Bengali texts along with English translations from Śrīla Prabhupāda's *Bhagavad-gītā As It Is*. To further reveal this gem in English, Svarūpa Krishna Prabhu of Kolkata painstakingly translated each word of *Gītār Gān* to English. If you're familiar with *Bhagavad-gītā As It Is*, you'll recognize dozens of fresh nuances and insights in *Gītār-gān*.

Gītār-gān uses two familiar Bengali rhyming patterns, mostly this common iambic couplet meter:

jaya jaya śrī-caitanya jaya nityānanda
jayādvaita-candra jaya gaura-bhakta-vṛnda

Occasionally, longer verses appear in this familiar Bengali pattern:

śrī-guru-caraṇa-padma, kevala-bhakati-sadma
bando mui sāvadhāna mate
jāhāra prasāde bhāi, e bhava toriyā jāi
kṛṣṇa-prāpti hoy jāhā ha'te

Verses in this longer pattern appear periodically through Śrīla Prabhupāda's Bengali text, generally corresponding with similarly long verses in the Sanskrit original.

If you're new to *Bhagavad-gītā*, we've included footnotes as an aid to your overall understanding of the text. Key Sanskrit names and phrases are numbered as they come up in the text and defined in the 'Endnotes' section. After enjoying this introductory version, you can dive deeper into self-realization by reading *Bhagavad-gītā As It Is*.

To the extent that we have accurately presented it, *Gītār-gān* will uplift you through the brilliant heart and mind of Śrīla Prabhupāda, an exemplary teacher and lover of the *Bhagavad-gītā*.

Kalakaṇṭha das, ACBSP

Chapter 1

The Yoga of Suffering and Distress

(viṣāda-yoga)

1) The doubtful Dhṛtarāṣtra said, "Sañjaya, please explain
what happened to my sons at holy Kurukṣetra's plain
when they attacked my brother Pāṇḍu's sons with all their might.
Describe the whole encounter when those warriors came to fight."

2) Sañjaya answered, "My dear King, please listen carefully.
Duryodhana, your mighty son, observed his enemies.
Assessing their formations, he decided to proceed
and tell his teacher Droṇācārya all that he had seen.[1]

3) *Duryodhana said:*
'My revered teacher, see the great militia that has come,
the army of the Pāndavas, arrayed by Drupad's son,
your competent disciple who now leads our enemies.
They're very tightly organized and powerful indeed.

4-6) 'Behold Bhīma and Arjuna, both archers of renown.
And equally accomplished are Virāt and Yuyudhān,
with Drupad and his sons and grandsons, highly skilled in war,
and Dhrṣṭaketu, Cekitāna, Kāśī's king and more.
Śaibya, Kuntibhoja and Purujit—do you see?

---

1 The *Bhagavad-gītā* was spoken just before a massive ancient battle at Kuruksetra in north-central India. The battle took place between the sons of Dhṛtarāṣtra and the sons of his brother Pāṇḍu. Prompted by his wicked son Duryodhana, the elderly Dhṛtarāṣtra had usurped Pāṇḍu's kingdom after Pāṇḍu unexpectedly died. Now Pāṇḍu's five sons, the Pandavas, stand ready to reclaim their rightful throne from the conniving sons of Dhṛtarāṣtra.

The two armies array themselves in strategic formations on the vast battlefield. When the anxious Dhṛtarāṣtra, who is blind, asks his secretary Sañjaya for a report, Sañjaya narrates the *Bhagavad-gītā*.

The *Bhagavad-gītā* is just one out of one hundred chapters in the epic *Mahabharata*. Although the warriors listed in this chapter all have fascinating backstories in the *Mahabharata*, knowing them is not necessary to benefit from the *Bhagavad-gītā*.

Yudhamanyu, who can fight extraordinarily?
And then there is Subhadrā's son and those of Draupadī.
These fighters and their chariots must all be given heed.

7) 'O best of brahmans, listen with great care as I describe
the mighty generals serving as the leaders for our side.
As you can see, our army is both powerful and vast,
an unending assembly of the finest warrior class.

8) 'Our best are you and Bhisma, flanked by Kripa, victors all.
Vikarṇa, Aśvatthāmā, Saumadattā wait our call.

9) 'A host of other heroes stand prepared to die for me.
My army, well-equipped and skilled, shall certainly succeed.

10, 11) 'Our power is unlimited with Bhīṣma in command,
while their force under Bhīma is severely undermanned.
O warriors! Take your given places on the battleground.
Make sure that Grandsire Bhisma is protected all around.'[2]

12) To hearten Duryodhan, the revered Bhīṣma, old but staunch,
released a lion's roaring sound by blowing on his conch.

13) The Kuru army, relishing this sound of victory
at once beat drums and sounded horns in great cacophony.

---

2 The arrogant and swaggering Duryodhana brags to his highly respected teacher Droṇācārya about his army, led by Bhīṣma, another venerated elder. Both Droṇācārya and Bhīṣma have been politically forced to fight for Duryodhana though their hearts are with the Pandavas.

14) Across the field were Krishna and Arjuna, seated tight
upon their chariot with horses all of flawless white.
They showed themselves prepared for war with conch blasts loud and long.
Then one by one came others in a great, transcendent song.

15) Hṛṣīkeśa, Lord Krishna, blew His conch named Pāñcajanya.
Dhanañjaya, Arjuna, then blew his, the Devadatta.
And Bhīmasen, who always managed herculean tasks,
then blew his conch, the Pauṇḍra, with a thunderous, booming blast.

16-18) The other Pāṇḍava conch shells resounded far and wide.
First Yudhisthir, the king, blew his, the Ananta-vijay.
Nakula blew the Sughoṣa, his celebrated shell.
His twin Sahadev blew the Maṇipuṣpaka as well.
Then Dhṛṣṭadyumna, Sātyaki, Virāṭa, Shikhaṇḍī,
and Abhimanyu, Kasiraj, the sons of Draupadī
all sounded their respective shells for all that they were worth,
creating a vibration that appeared to shake the Earth.

19) The sons and friends of Dhṛtarāṣtra on the other side
all felt their hearts were shattered as that sound ripped through the sky.

20) Arjuna saw the mighty Kuru battlement array,
yet Hanumān[I] upon his banner left him unafraid.
His hands upon his bow and arrows, set to do his part,
he called out to Lord Krishna, ever-present in his heart.[3]

3 Among the Pandavas, and among all the warriors, Arjuna was known as the best archer.

21-23) ‘Drive us between the armies now, my dear, unfailing friend.
Approach the many enemies with whom I must contend.
I wish to see these soldiers who have come here so inclined
to satisfy the sons of Dhṛtarāṣhtra’s evil minds.’

24, 25) On hearing this, Hṛṣīkeśa[II] respectfully complied
and steered that best of chariots between the warring sides.
On seeing Bhīṣma, Droṇā, Dhṛtarāṣhtra’s sons and more,
Lord Krishna said, ‘Behold the fighters gathered for this war.’

26) Arjuna saw a gathering of loving, caring guides,
relations and respected elders standing on both sides.
He saw his sons and grandsons set to fight against his friends.
The massive group of loved ones seemed expanded without end.

27) To see these relatives made Pārtha[III] tremble with distress.
At once his state of mind became exceedingly depressed.
His taste for fighting vanished and his heart gave way to dread.
Compassion made him cry. He turned to Krishna as he said,

28) “On seeing friends and relatives enticed to battle here,
my limbs are shaking, and my sense of taste has disappeared.

29) ‘My bow Gāṇḍīva slips from my unsteady, trembling hand.
It feels as if a burning arrow strikes me where I stand,
consuming all my skin and bones in flames that have no end.
Do not go. No, do not go any further, my dear friend.

30) A triumph seems like loss in my chaotic mental state.
O Keshava[IV], this war is a disaster, a mistake.

31) O Krishna, drive me back. What good is killing off my kin?
How could we gain a joyous, peaceful kingdom in the end?

32-35) What happiness can royal life or peace or money yield
if those for whom we wish them fight and die upon this field?
I see our teachers, fathers, sons, the fathers of our wives,
our grandfathers and grandsons, all prepared to give their lives.
Our brothers-in-law, uncles, all these loved ones so revered—
if we proceed to battle, they will leave their bodies here.
Their deaths would be far more than I have strength enough to see.
Much better for us all if death would simply come to me.
Janārdana[V], if even all three worlds were somehow won,
what pleasure would I gain by killing Dhṛtarāśtra's sons?

36) What soldier fights opposing armies formed of friends and kin?
If we kill them, our profit shall be nothing more than sin.
If all the sons of Dhṛtarāśtra and their friends were slain,
how could we feel the slightest joy? Regret is all we'd gain.

37, 38) Though greed leads them to think it is auspicious now to fight
and kill so many relatives, does that mean it is right?
Just who would bear the burden of this devastating fault?
Is it not better to avoid a sin and its results?
This war would mean disaster and destroy our royal line.
Janārdana, O Krishna, what could counteract this crime?

39) When royal dynasties collapse, eternal *dharma*[4] falls,
which leaves only *adharma* to contaminate us all.

40, 41) *Adharma* growing prominent means women are defiled,
producing unplanned children, undesired, running wild.
Unwanted populations then create a hell for all.
It seems these killers want our royal family to fall.

42) Our forefathers no longer would receive their offerings,
the only means for us to be relieved of suffering.
Unwanted children would then devastate our great tradition
of welfare work uplifting our community's position.

43) Uprooting one's familial line, as I have heard from saints,
would be accepted only by those men who lack restraint.
Janārdana, O Krishna, all the saints assert as well
that family-killers lose all happiness and go to hell.

44) Alas, alas, we are degraded, planning a great sin.
It's surely wrong to claim a throne by killing off one's kin.

45) If Dhritarastra's sons attack they'll kill me here, unarmed.
I think I'll wait for death instead of causing any harm.'

46) Arjuna, having spoken on his chariot, sat still.
And there, upon the battlefield, despite his famous skills,
he put aside his weapons and decided to be kind
as misery and anguish overwhelmed his troubled mind."

4 *Dharma* in this case means one's pious religious duty. *Adharma* is the opposite.

Bhaktivedanta Swami thus recites śrī-gītār gān
to please the pure devotees always rapt in Krishna's song.

Thus ends the first chapter of Śrimad Bhagavad-gītā *named* viṣāda-yoga,
the yoga of suffering and distress.

Chapter 2

Knowledge of the Soul and Body by Analytical Study

(Sāṅkhya-yoga)

1) *Sanjaya said*:

Arjuna, shedding tears of pity, thoroughly confused,
heard Madhusūdan[VI] speak with sweet and friendly attitude.

2) *Lord Krishna said*:

My dear Arjuna, why shed tears upon this field of war?
A foolish man laments for values wiser men abhor.
Your tears lead not to heaven but to widespread disrepute.
My friend, you must abandon this misplaced, degraded mood.

3) Why should this lack of potency degrade your martial skill?
A feeble-hearted soldier is unfit to fight and kill.
My friend, how has this weak behavior set you so far back?
How will you counteract your fearsome enemy's attack?

4) *Arjuna said*:

O Killer of the Madhu beast, I can't imagine why
You want my lethal arrows to take revered elders' lives.
Why should I pierce my learned gurus' flesh as You have said?
I'd rather worship Bhīṣmadev's and Droṇa's feet instead.

5) They're more than military guides.
They're saintly souls and very wise.
My friend, You think I should kill those I love?
Why, I would rather beg for bread
than fight till they or I am dead.
What profit lies in winnings stained with blood?

6) Should I kill them, or they kill me?
I'm caught in a dichotomy,
as if a man with feet on separate rafts.
To kill my friends who will not run
and Dhṛtarāśtra's hostile sons
assures us only sorrow unsurpassed.

7) I feel so weak with meager vision,
baffled in my comprehension.
Only fools abandon sacred posts.
Now let the whole world witness You
tell me the proper thing to do.
Please help me be determined and composed.

8) So blind of eye and dull of brain,
I'm too impure to douse the flames
of pain that burn my senses and my poise.
For even with unrivaled throne
or heaven's kingdom as my own,
how can this sorrow ever be destroyed?

9) *Sanjaya said*:
Reflecting thus, Arjuna, always self-controlled and strong,
again said, 'Krishna, master of desire, this is wrong.
Govinda, pleaser of the senses, I shall quit this war.'
With that, the sullen hero sat and offered nothing more.

10) On hearing this, with gentle smile, between the warring sides,
Lord Krishna gave his stricken friend the following advice.

11) *Lord Krishna said*:
Although your words are learned, you lament for something lame.
The truly learned know that soul and body aren't the same.
The body dies but spirit lives, and clearly judging this,
the wise do not lament the body's certain exodus.

12) For you and I and all these kings have passed through countless lives.
We all exist eternally, yet fools think otherwise.

13) The soul and body differ, as the paṇḍits have explained.
The endless soul remains untouched as fleeting bodies change.
Through childhood, youth and aged years, the soul lives on and on
and goes on living even when the body's dead and gone.

14) As winter turns to summer, joy and sorrow come and go.
A man attached to sense perceptions wavers as they flow.
Attachment to the temporary must be overcome.
When one learns to be tolerant, attachment will succumb.

15) A person who appreciates the goal of life attains
a tolerant position that surpasses joy and pain.
Such persons remain steady in a world of agitation,
forsaking temporary things for endless liberation.

16) The seers of the truth conclude, by studying in full
the qualities of both the body and the spirit soul,
that bodies are ephemeral, but spirits never die.
Conclusions such as this alone can benefit mankind.

17) The endless soul pervades the body, making one aware.
Without the soul, the body falls and can't move anywhere.
The soul goes on forever, as concluded by the wise,
for how can one destroy or murder that which never dies?

18) The body surely perishes, but one must also know
there is no end to the immortal, boundless spirit soul.
Discerning this reality as proper, true, and right,
stand up to face this war and with determination, fight.

19) A person who thinks souls can kill or be killed is misled.
No one can kill the spirit soul, for souls are never dead.

20) The soul transcends mortality.
It was, it is, and it will be.
The soul is both beginningless and old.
The endless and undying soul
cannot be born, cannot be culled,
for only bodies die, not spirit souls.

21) Now why would one who knows the soul is indestructible
imagine he can kill someone or cause someone to kill?

If one sees souls are everywhere and present all the time,
unlike a foolish man, he knows that souls can never die.

22) As any person puts on clothes
brand-new and fresh, discarding those
worn out and old and no longer of use,
at mortal death the soul again
assumes another untouched skin.
Regretting death in war is no excuse.

23) The soul cannot be burned or drowned or changed by worldly force.
No weapon can impale the soul; no wind blows it off course.
Wise hero, such intrusions only touch the outer form.
They're actions and reactions of this world and nothing more.

24) The soul has bliss that never breaks or withers or evolves,
unlike something material that flounders and dissolves.
The spirit soul's pervasive presence stays forever fresh,
unfettered and unchanging although physically enmeshed.

25) Assaulting, burning, moistening, and drying just affect
the body that repeatedly departs and manifests.
While human minds can fathom qualities material,
the spiritual existence remains inconceivable.
The changeless nature of the soul so differs from the skin
that one must hear of soul and flesh again and yet again.
When you see how they differ and can set the two apart,
that new discrimination will exhilarate your heart.

26) When you can see the soul lives on, you will lament no more.
Your lasting bliss will far surpass what you have known before.
Yet if, 'The body is the self,' remains your firm belief
and death means one is gone for good, there's still no need for grief.

27) Since bodies die and turn again to earthly elements
that form another body, learned souls do not lament.

28) If matter forms a body and some fleeting traits appear,
the soulless remained soulless all along. Why shed a tear?

29) Knowledge of the soul amazes.
Contacting the soul amazes.
Once perceived, the soul makes one enthralled.
Some declare the soul amazes.
Some have heard the soul amazes.
Most don't know the soul exists at all.

30) O Bhārata[VII], to hear and learn about the spirit soul
comprises the epitome of all the Vedic scrolls.
In My view, all embodied souls endure their body's death,
so grieving over this destruction simply wastes your breath.[5]

5 Krishna presents the first, foundational lesson of *Bhagavad-gītā*: the soul lives apart from the physical body. To know this and act accordingly, Krishna insists, immediately takes one to bliss and steadiness missing from ordinary, body-centered lives. Unlike the gross material elements that comprise the body, the spirit is a subtle, non-material element, invisible to ordinary vision yet perceivable by intelligence. Having established this framework, Krishna proceeds to appeal to the warrior Arjuna's pride.

31) Since every righteous person has a duty to fulfill,
a *kṣatriya*[VIII] must never hesitate to fight and kill.

32) The doors of heaven open wide when one does not neglect
to meet the sacred duties that society expects.
Not only do heroic warriors reach the gods' domains,
their sacrifice brings fortune that heroic men obtain.

33) So, if you leave your sacred role of fighting in this war,
O Pārtha, you will lose the fame you've always known before.

34) The world will sing and laugh about your cowardice, your shame,
and think of you as dead. Your life will never be the same.

35) The great opposing soldiers who have long admired your power
will see you flee the battle and declare you are a coward.

36) What benefit will come if you are harshly criticized?
O Pārtha, will you listen as you hide in some disguise?

37) If you survive you will enjoy this worldly sovereignty,
and if you die then heaven shall become your destiny.
Kaunteya[IX], either way, to stay is surely good and right.
Your negligence surprises Me. The time has come to fight.[6]

6 Having appealed to Arjuna's intellect with knowledge of the soul and the warrior's duty, Krishna now introduces *karma-yoga*, the art of working without attachment. Most of the topics introduced in this chapter will be later be explained in more depth.

38) In joy or sorrow, loss or profit, triumph or defeat,
be fearless in your work and disregard what others speak.
Just fight for fighting's sake and sin will always stay aloof.
You have no need to fear if you can grasp this vital truth.

39) Thus far I have explained how to use knowledge as a guide.
Now learn how one can work more wisely, motives set aside.
Those souls of ripened intellect choose serving the Supreme
and free themselves from bondage caused by acting in a dream.

40) Now in this practice no decay, no loss or cost occurs,
and any service you amass is wealth forever yours.
A slight amount of progress in your service can avert
exposure to the greatest fear, repeated death and birth.

41) Beloved Kuru child, determined servitors possess
both resolute intention and unbound intelligence.
But others lack persistent drive to serve the Absolute,
for many-branched intelligence makes them irresolute.

42, 43) The flowery Vedic themes cheer mundane worker's hearts and minds
by promising sweet pleasures and enjoyment of all kinds.
Although the pleasures they pursue all vanish in the end,
such lusty persons try to rise to heaven once again.
In sole pursuit of promises of heavenly delights
they fail to link with God, the single goal of human life.

44) Beset with thousands of desires, mental balance shot,
they find the will for serving God a distant afterthought.
They stay attached to pleasure, mystic powers, or salvation
and never reach devotion with a fixed determination.[7]

45) The modes of goodness, dark and passion fill the Vedic texts.
Transcend their worldly influence and vanquish their effects.
You'll then achieve pure goodness, free of all dualities,
and grow attached to treasures of divine affinity.

46) Though water is the same in every well and every river,
a single river gives what many, many wells deliver.
And so, the varied meanings of the Vedic texts' commands
are singular, as *brāhmans* who love God can understand.

47) You have the right to do your work as you are best employed,
yet all the fruits of what you do are not yours to enjoy.
Think not yourself the doer nor the owner of your yield
and you shall find things favorable working in your field.

48) Detached from fruits, the yogi does his duty to please God,
regardless, Dhanañjaya, if it's perfect or it's flawed.
So do your duty like the steady yogi and you'll find
you'll fully satisfy the mystic longings of your mind.

---

7 While the Vedic literatures describe options for pious, detached work in pursuit of money, prestige and pleasure, Krishna advises Arjuna to step up to devotional service to the Supreme. Such service includes detachment, but also leads to lasting fulfillment, unlike the ephemeral results of Vedic rituals.

49) If you decide to see your lust for worldliness destroyed,
self-centered, Godless actions are the actions to avoid.
One's miserly possessiveness is instantly redeemed
when one becomes surrendered to the will of the Supreme.

50) By serving the Supreme a person's actions become cleansed.
Reactions, pious and impious, soon come to an end.
While fighting thus, your consciousness surpasses the mundane
and work becomes the art of yoga on a higher plane.

51) Great saints and sages do their work in this enlightened mood,
renouncing selfish actions and reactions that accrue.
Renounced and transcendental, all such yogis come to see
a liberated state of life devoid of misery.

52) When transcendental service lifts your mind above the dream
that body is the self, a farce that muddies everything,
you too shall be indifferent to lust in all its forms
as well as all the Vedic hymns you hear or heard before.

53) When lesser Vedic messages no longer move your mind
your knowledge and your actions will successfully align
with service to the Absolute. No method passes this,
the highest state of yoga and transcendent consciousness.[8]

---

8 In his *Bhagavad-gītā As It Is*, Śrila Prabhupāda entitles this lengthy chapter, "Contents of the *Gītā* Summarized." Krishna has identified the soul, appealed to Arjuna's martial pride, described detached work (*karma-yoga*), and introduced devotional service (*bhakti-yoga*). He now concludes by describing the enlightened *bhakti-yogi*.

54) *Arjuna said*:
O Keśava, now tell me of transcendence if You please.
How does a transcendental person walk or sit at ease?
A man of fixed intelligence—what language does he speak?
What other qualities make this accomplished soul unique?

55) *Lord Krishna said*:
When one gives up concocted sense impulses and perceives
how soul and Supersoul relate, he's satisfied and pleased.
While he progresses, others, keen on sensual pursuit,
just suffer on and on from that deficient substitute.

56) A man whose mind is peaceful both in misery and joy,
whose service in devotion keeps him constantly employed,
relieved of any craving, sorrow, fretfulness, or rage,
is known to everybody as a steady-minded sage.

57) A person who forgets about the physical demands,
receiving good and evil without praise or reprimand,
devoid of hatred, showing much goodwill to all he meets,
is known to be a steady soul whose knowledge is complete.

58) While servants of the senses suffer unceasing distress,
the masters of the senses keep a sober consciousness.
Like turtles tugging tender limbs within a solid shell,
they keep demands for sense enjoyment tucked away and quelled.
Thus wise, consistent persons who are fixed in self-control
are known to be *goswamis*, realized, liberated souls.

59) Reducing sense enjoyment, though, is not at all the same,
for those who have true knowledge keep a different mental frame.
By tasting transcendental bliss one naturally eschews
the mundane pleasures gleaned from common sensual pursuits.

60) Yes, even learned souls who try to keep their senses checked
will find them too impetuous and strong in all respects.
Devoid of sacred pleasure, dry denial will produce
a fire on the forehead, throwing childish minds askew.

61) So, one who serves the Absolute and regulates each sense
is certainly a person of secure intelligence.

62-63) To dryly give up sense objects will make a person's mind
recall their thrill and tend to dwell upon them all the time.
These contemplated cravings generate a burning lust
that then goes unfulfilled and turns to fury and disgust.
Bewildered by this anger, one forgets his higher views,
and, losing his intelligence, he lapses into ruin.

64) Much better one should act without attachment or aversion
and quickly break this endless round of sensual diversions.
Their consciousness enriched with special grace from the Supreme,
such persons remain active in this world and yet are free.

65) Relief from all attachment causes miseries to end,
and by the grace of God, transcendent happiness descends.

A person with this mercy and whose consciousness is fixed
can live with wisdom even in a world of ignorance.

66) Though nature blesses every soul with joyful consciousness,
if one does not serve God, one never seems to find such bliss.
A selfish, thoughtless state of mind makes discontent increase,
for how can one be happy when one's mind is not at peace?

67) One's sensual desires toss one on the mental plane
as if one were a rowboat tumbling in a hurricane.
A person uncontrolled is lost, like boats within a storm,
for constant uproar won't let their intelligence perform.

68) O mighty-armed Arjuna, therefore, listen well to Me.
A person who submits their mind to serving the Supreme
will always keep their senses well controlled in such pursuit
and bolster their intelligence as firm and resolute.

69) While worldly people chase sense objects through their wakeful days
the godly people, calm as night, keep sense desire at bay.
The godly people waken to the daylight of the soul,
while worldly people's spirits sleep through nighttime, dark and cold.

70) A mighty, endless river flows forever to the sea,
which takes in water undisturbed, not changing one degree.
So also does a godly person feel the flow of lust,
yet due to sacred practices, can peacefully adjust.

71) A godly soul like Nārada, whose lust is fully tamed,
can wander everywhere to sing and praise God's holy names.
Released from all material attachments and conceits,
such persons become sages as they relish endless peace.

72) For sages with divine remembrance, spiritually infused,
how can illusion linger on and leave the mind confused?
Such saintly souls are so steadfast, above the grip of time,
that even at the hour of death they keep a peaceful mind.

Bhaktivedanta Swami thus recites śrī-gītār gān
to please the pure devotees always rapt in Krishna's song.

Thus ends the second chapter of Śrimad Bhagavad-gītā *named* sāṅkhya-yoga, *descriptive knowledge of the soul and the body by analytical study.*

Chapter 3

Discharge of One's Prescribed Duty of Devotional Service to the Supreme Lord

(Karma-yoga)

1) *Arjuna said*:
If yoga is a higher goal of life than worldly gain,
why would You occupy me in this ghastly war campaign?

2) These contradictory instructions leave me more confused.
Now tell me please, decisively, which option I should choose.

3) *Lord Krishna said*:
As I have said, two kinds of faithful people look for truth.
Some people practice yoga, and some seek empiric proof.[9]

4) A man who gives up righteous duties he has been prescribed
imagines he is karma-free but really acts from pride.
To simply put off doing work to which one is assigned
will neither bring perfection nor transparency of mind.

5) At every moment, by one's natural propensity,
one cannot stop performing some innate activity.
And everybody's natural and unrestricted acts
will place them into bondage to reactions coming back.

6) When fools refrain from pleasures that they contemplate within,
their yoga is ensnared. The scriptures say they just pretend.

7) Instead, control your senses with a purpose to progress,
and step by step the crazy monkey mind will acquiesce.

---

9 Krishna now addresses Arjuna's question by explaining that working for the Supreme is the same as acting in knowledge. Thus he defeats Arjuna's notion of quitting his work for a sentimental ideal.

The Lord protects such yogis who externally maintain,
yet stay detached within by working on a higher plane.

8) To execute one's duties far surpasses sitting still,
for those who give up work will find their bodies frail and ill.
Such people think themselves renounced, while all they've done, in fact,
is set upon themselves a foolish, self-defeating act.

9) Detached and regulated duties pleasing *Bhagavān*[X]
are offered as a sacrifice and sever karmic bonds.
By simply working in this way your freedom is assured,
but working without sacrifice constrains one to this world.[10]

10) The Lord of every creature gave His subjects sacrifice
and blessed them all by saying, "This procedure will suffice
to bring you to a happy life with all that you require
to satisfy your senses and supply what you desire."

11) The demigods[XI], responsible for all necessities,
accept the sacrifices of mankind and thus are pleased.
In turn, they make sure mankind suffers no deficiency.
These mutual exchanges will assure prosperity.

12) The demigods, content with mankind's sacrifice, provide
the foodstuffs and all else required to keep men satisfied.

10 In response to Arjuna asking whether yoga is superior to work, Krishna explains that work, though inevitable, can be turned into yoga through sacrifice.

But if a person simply eats to give himself relief
without returning sacrifice, he's no more than a thief.

13) When one eats foodstuffs left from sacrificial presentation,
he sheds his sins and walks upon the path of liberation.
But when one eats to simply satisfy his own desires,
he suffers through the burden of the sin that he acquires.

14) One lives by eating food grains, which are born of falling rain.
The rains are caused by sacrifice, which righteous work maintains.

15) Prescribed and righteous work, the Vedas say, has come from God,
while other work is mental fabrication, a façade.
The duties one performs are meant to worship the Supreme,
the all-pervading Lord of sacrificial work's regime.

16) If one avoids this cycle of transcendent sacrifice,
one misses Vedic guidance that is meant for human life.
Such persons seek out nothing more than sensual delight,
that leads them to incessant sin, anxiety, and fright.

17) A man who knows the self, however, has no obligation
except for serving God in full and pleasing realization.

18) The Vedas say a realized soul performs his work and yet
will never judge an action based on what he plans to get.
A truly selfless person thus retains no earthly debt,
for selfless work brings benefits he never can forget.

19) Thus, selfless and detached, one simply works as he's obliged
and benefits by reaching, step by step, the feet of God.

20) The saintly king named Janaka through duty gained perfection,
and you should do the same to give the common man direction.
A monkey has no duty but to procreate and play,
and nobody can benefit renouncing in that way.

21) A great man's noble actions leave the common people stirred,
while vile men's actions strike them both as foolish and absurd.
Whatever standards noble people set become well known
in cities, towns, and villages, in everybody's home.

22) O son of Pṛthā, note that I have no prescribed routine
in worlds below or worlds above or anywhere between.
Nor is there any single thing I hanker to possess,
and yet you see I always do My duty, nonetheless.

23) For if I ever failed to do My duties as assigned,
the population of the world would follow right behind.

24) If I shirked duties, no one would do work they could avoid.
All standards would be broken, and the world will be destroyed.

25) The learned do their work and are attached, so it appears,
so fools, who really are attached, will carry on with theirs.

26) Instead of just disrupting those with selfish, foolish minds,
the wise lead by example and give tasks of better kinds.

27) The learned and the foolish hold completely different views
on whether they are souls or are the flesh the soul imbues.
Misled by such false ego, fools imagine they control
activities the modes of nature force upon their souls.

28) The knowers of the Absolute see this essential fact:
the modes of nature influence the sensuous to act.
A gentle person therefore always shuns the selfish way
of working for material results the senses crave.

29) Bewildered by the modes of nature, fools are firmly tied
to actions they believe will make their senses satisfied.
Affected as they are, such foolish people, nonetheless,
should be engaged in work by which they gradually progress.

30) So Pārtha, therefore give your strength to God and not to pride.
Just fight and set your foolish, selfish, stingy plans aside.

31) In My view, those who execute their work for the Supreme,
and worship Lord Hari[XII] with humble, dutiful routines
that make them both devoted and more spiritually absorbed,
are freed from the attachment to the fruits their work awards.

32) But others who submit themselves to nature's modes pursue
ambitions tied to nature's ebb and flow in all they do.

33) And from time immemorial, attached, dependent souls
forever stay engrossed in matter, helplessly controlled.

34) So, give up taste and distaste for the objects of the senses.
Detached and calm, your service to Lord Mādhava[XIII] commences.

35) It's best to do your own work, not the work of someone else,
regardless if your duty might bring death upon yourself.
By doing your own duty as a gift to the Supreme,
you link with God in yoga through the deepest of all means.[11]

36) *Arjuna said*:
O Vārṣṇeya,[XIV] please clarify this mystery for me:
why do the living beings seem to sin obsessively?
What overwhelming power leads a soul to awful deeds
that violate his judgment, his desires, and his needs?"

37) *Lord Krishna said*:
The mode of passion leads to lust that later turns to wrath
and leaves all souls throughout three worlds in baffled aftermath.
To wiser persons are these two great enemies exposed,
and hence they act with caution and transcend the lower modes.

---

11 Krishna has now explained how Arjuna's initial idea to renounce the battle reflected an ignorant concept of renunciation. Intelligent people fulfill their duties and attain renunciation by offering their work and its fruits to the Supreme.

Krishna has hinted about His own position as the Supreme Personality of Godhead, but Arjuna wants to know more about what causes people to abandon their real self-interest and chase sense pleasure.

38) Throughout the worlds this lust prevails and covers living beings,
who do not see how lust is thus involved in everything.
As wombs obscure their embryos or smoke surrounds a fire,
all souls are covered over by their lusty sense desires.

39) The endless enemy of lust obscures the spotless soul,
relentless, never sated, always keeping him controlled.
Since lust is like an all-pervading, ever-burning blaze,
a thoughtful man is cautious in the way that he behaves.

40) That lust resides within one's senses, mind, and intellect
and keeps one in a dreamworld with illusory effect.
That lust creates the false belief that body is the self
which makes one feel autonomous and overrate oneself.

41) O son of Bhārat, therefore from the very start you must
be dutiful and unattached and regulate this lust.
To serve God with devotion will empower you to slay
this lust, the bane of wisdom. There is just no other way.

42) The senses govern matter, and the mind controls each sense.
The soul surpasses mind because it rules intelligence.
And thus, for the conditioned soul, the wisest protocol
is service to the Supersoul, who stands above them all.

43) Such service, born of sacred wisdom, thoroughly removes
both lust and consequent illusion. Thus, one can improve.

For only through such service to the Lord with heart and soul
can lust, the tireless enemy, be conquered and controlled.

Bhaktivedanta Swami thus recites śrī-gītār gān
to please the pure devotees always rapt in Krishna's song.

Thus ends the third chapter of Śrimad Bhagavad-gītā *named* karma-yoga *or discharge of one's prescribed duty of devotional service to the Supreme Lord.*

Chapter 4

Transcendental Knowledge

(jñana-yoga)

1) *Krishna said:*

In ages past I also spoke about the wondrous theme
of how to offer selfless work by serving the Supreme.
I taught the sun god Surya, who taught Manu, his own son,
who then taught King Ikṣvāku as the lineage went on.

2) Throughout successive generations, saintly monarchs heard
this same *Bhagavad-gītā*, every lesson, every word.
The chain went on unbroken till the influence of time
corrupted all the knowledge and destroyed the ancient line.

3) Today, therefore, I'll teach you of man's link with the Divine
and resurrect this lineage to benefit mankind.
For who can know the truth without a sacred serving mood?
My friend, today this mystery shall be explained to you.

4) *Arjuna said:*

But you are very young, a man of modest years, my friend,
and Surya's years, in millions, surely number in the tens.
In light of your respective ages, I don't comprehend
how you could have instructed him back then as you contend.[12]

5) *Lord Krishna said:*

Arjuna, you and I have passed through many, many lives.
Though you do not remember them, My memory survives.

---

12 As Einstein posits in his Special Theory of Relativity, the rate at which time passes depends on your frame of reference. For demigods such as Surya, human years are but moments. Since Arjuna has asked about Surya's and Krishna's respective ages, Krishna now directly discloses His position as the Supreme Personality of Godhead.

This lapse is due to your condition as a living being,
but I have no such limits. I remember everything.

6) My unborn body, unlike others, never fades away.
Though I exist as Supersoul in every time and place,
by My inherent energy, I choose to reappear
in My sublime, transcendent form. You see, that's why I'm here.

7) Whenever and wherever righteous principles decay,
and in their place, unrighteous principles predominate,
O Bharata, I manifest Myself in forms diverse,
reducing evil burdens placed upon the universe.

8) Delivering the pious souls who walk the path of truth
and vanquishing impious souls of foul, profane pursuits,
I come Myself to reestablish true morality
in era after era. You must know this factually.

9) For one who understands My birth and actions as divine,
good fortune manifests and generates a life sublime.
When such great persons leave their bodies, they at once attain
relief from further birth as they return to My domain.

10) Renouncing useless moods of anger, fearfulness, and greed,
so many learned souls have grown absorbed in serving Me.
Devoted souls thus open wide the gates to purity,
attaining Me and giving up corrupt activity.

11) As someone worships Me, I give results accordingly.
If one pursues in Me their safe and sole security,
they quickly gain My shelter as their reservations lapse.
Regardless of their purpose, everyone is on My path.

12) For mystic skills and profit, men serve gods in many ways.
Such quick rewards soon disappear, resulting in dismay.

13) For humans, I have made a sacred four-fold social system[13]
according to their actions under nature's supervision.
Though I create the force of nature, it does not touch Me,
for I am in control of everyone's activities.

14) The fruits of action never impact Me at any time,
nor do I want results from any act of any kind.
If one can understand these truths regarding what I do
one also frees oneself from action's karmic residue.

15) The sages of the past who learned these secret words of truth
were also freed of bondage to their actions and their fruits.
If you will simply follow previous authorities,
you too will reach perfection in significant degrees.[14]

16) Since even sages cannot fathom action and inaction,
I'll now explain and ease your hardship and dissatisfaction.

---

13 Krishna explains this social system, known as *varnashram dharma*, in 18.41-44.

14 Having introduced the identity of the Supreme, Krishna now explains how serving the Supreme automatically results in detachment.

17) Your knowledge is perfected when you clearly understand
both action and inaction and those actions that are banned.
Although it may be difficult to know these mysteries,
if one succeeds, he comes to see a core reality.

18) The wise can see inaction even in activity,
as well as action taking place while sitting restfully.

19) A man whose every action is devoid of sense desire
burns sin, the learned say, for perfect knowledge is like fire.

20) Abandoning attachment to the fruits of every deed,
a person remains blissful and is satisfied indeed.
Such people freely act and move about the world and yet
they do their duties unattached to anything they get.

21) Detached in mind and intellect, the wise, in all respects,
renounce the sense of ownership of all that they possess.
Dynamic and yet acting just to simply keep their health,
such persons give up karmic deeds and thus advance themselves.

22) Content with any benefit that naturally accrues,
relieved of all duality and jealous attitudes,
consistent in intelligence and duties to be done,
one finishes both karma and disdain for anyone.

23) No longer mixed with nature's modes, the wise remain serene,
enlightened with full knowledge of the soul and the Supreme.
They expertly serve God on all occasions and attain,
by practice, full immersion on the transcendental plane.

24) Because of constant acts of spiritual integrity,
the work that one performs becomes an offering of ghee
into the fire of sacrifice, consumed by the Supreme.
Triumphant and absorbed, one gains the Absolute regime.[15]

25) Some yogis worship demigods with various oblations,
while others sacrifice to My Brahman[XV] manifestation.

26) The unadulterated *brahmacārīs*[XVI] sacrifice
their senses in the fire their ascetic minds ignite.
And some submit sense objects such as feeling, sound and taste
as sacrifices offered in the fire of restraint.

27) Some yogīs give their life air and the functions of each sense
as sacrifices in the flames of mastered consciousness.
Such persons separate themselves from urges and desires,
acquiring knowledge after which they carefully aspired.

28) Some yogīs read the Vedas, others give up all possessions,
while some use mystic yoga and still others strict repression.

15 Krishna now lists a variety of paths yogis take in pursuit of transcendental knowledge.

29) Still others practice breath restraint to help themselves advance.
By merging in- and outward breath, they maintain mystic trance.
Such yogīs reduce eating, finding breathing will suffice
while offering their very breath itself as sacrifice.

30) These many types of learned yogīs step by step begin
to free themselves from sinful deeds and grow completely cleansed.
Becoming deeply faithful with a taste for sacrifice,
they qualify to gain Supreme, eternal, sinless life.

31) In this world or in this life or in lifetimes subsequent,
if one abandons sacrifice, how can one be content?

32) O best of men, all *dharma* lives in sacrifice alone,
for sacrifice is all the Vedic wisdom texts condone.
Ascribed to varied work and many-branched though it may be,
it's sacrifice that ultimately sets a person free.

33) And yet the sacrifice of knowledge surely is the best.
It far surpasses simply giving up what you possess.
Such knowledge comes from action that's devoid of expectation,
a practice of the mind that will resolve contamination.

34) Take shelter of a guru so your knowledge is complete.
Give service and submissively inquire at his feet.
A guru who is qualified and equal to the task
will give this knowledge just to benefit whoever asks.

35) A realized person gives up the illusory response
of happiness in victory and agony in loss.
Relieved of these dualities, one comes to comprehend
that God is always present, and all souls are linked to Him.

36) For even the most sinful sinner, knowledge is the ship
that helps him sail across illusion's unremitting grip.

37) As logs are turned to ashes when they're tossed in blazing fire,
ones' karma is destroyed as sacred knowledge is acquired.
The mundane knowledge of the so-called learned can't compare,
for it will never purify and helps but here and there.

38) When yogis reach maturity, their lives are full of bliss,
for transcendental knowledge makes one pure in consciousness.

39) A faithful soul with knowledge and with senses pacified
at once attains serenity as miseries subside.

40) But faithless persons, foolishly ignoring sacred texts,
fall down to bonds of suffering in this life and the next.

41) This sacrifice for the Supreme will scatter all one's doubts
as transcendental knowledge comes progressively about.
When one becomes self-situated, karma is erased.
O Dhanañjaya, you can also reach this sacred place.

42) These many heartfelt doubts that are arising within you
are born from your illusion and your unenlightened views.
Awake to transcendental knowledge, slash your worries down.
Be fixed in yoga in this world. Get up and stand your ground.

Bhaktivedanta Swami thus recites śrī-gītār gān
to please the pure devotees always rapt in Krishna's song.

Thus ends the fourth chapter of Śrimad Bhagavad-gītā *named* jñana-yoga *or transcendental knowledge.*

Chapter 5

Action in Kṛṣṇa Consciousness

(karma-sannyāsa-yoga)

1) *Arjuna said:*
O Krishna, first You say that one should seek renunciation,
then You describe God's service as a better situation.
Now of the two, do You know which is definitely best?
If so, then please explain and help me put my doubts to rest.[16]

2) *Lord Krishna said:*
Though Vedic texts praise each approach for spiritual promotion,
an active person won't neglect to work in pure devotion.

3) By working in devotion without loathing or desire,
detached from sense enjoyment, in pursuit of something higher,
one casts away dualities, entanglements, and grief.
O mighty-armed Arjuna, this is My assured belief.

4) Since serving God and *sāṅkhya*[XVII] studies both lead to perfection,
a childish fool alone divides devotion from discretion.

5) An analytic overview, as *sāṅkhya* advocates,
like working in devotion, will perfect the candidate.
Thus, *sāṅkhya* or devotion, with applied intelligence,
will lead to understandings of an equal consequence.

6) The soul who merely gives up work and does not work for God
has uselessly embraced a false renunciate's façade.

---

16 Having described transcendental knowledge (*jñāna yoga*), Krishna now connects it to devotion (*bhakti yoga*).

O mighty armed Arjuna, perfect, thoughtful souls engaged
in serving the Supreme achieve His feet without delay.

7) To serve in pure devotion purifies and guarantees
that one controls the senses and sheds lower qualities.
Such expert persons give up sense desires in themselves
while working to bring benefit to everybody else.[17]

8,9) True yogis know that all they do, they do not really do,
like touching, hearing, seeing, breathing, dreaming, taking food,
conversing and enjoying things or giving things away,
accompanied, alone, asleep, or rising for the day.
Although their senses do such work like everybody else,
within, the yogi always meditates upon the Self.

10) By serving the Supreme and doing duties selflessly,
untouched by sense enjoyment or by sin and piety,
a realized person acts without anxiety and fear.
Like lotus leaves untouched by water, nothing interferes.

11) The wise work in devotion with the body, words, and mind,
while those of misplaced intellect are sensually inclined.
The yogi in devotion is renounced and well aware
that he links with divinity in service everywhere.

---

17 Krishna now describes in detail the enlightened, knowledgeable yogi who comes to full spiritual life through devotion.

12) By giving up the fruits of work and acting in devotion,
a yogi gains unflinching peace amid this world's commotion.
In contrast, those who work in lust for outcomes that they seek
cannot renounce and stay entangled, frustrated, and weak.

13) Fulfilling all external duties, keeping peace inside,
this unattached and active person happily resides
within the body physical, the city of nine gates.
Such flawless souls work selflessly and never abdicate.

14) A soul long having fallen in the endless worldly ocean
does not create the fruits of work, in greed or in devotion.
The three modes of material complexity ordain
the fruits of all activities within this realm of pain.

15) The Lord does not create the soul's endeavors, vile or pious,
for souls act for enjoyment due to ignorance and bias.
And when the soul pursues enticing sensual displays,
illusion, *māyā*, waiting, takes him captive right away.

16) When knowledge is developed, therefore, *māyā* loses sway.
The soul, enlightened, then resumes its own inherent ways,
exactly as the darkness in the nighttime is undone
before the shining brilliance of the rising morning sun.

17) Then wisdom, faith and knowledge become helpful, realized themes
that free one from illusion to be rapt in the Supreme.

18) Enlightened souls will come to see with vision fair and equal
a cow, a dog, an elephant, and great or lowly people,
including learned *brāhmaṇas* of wise and gentle mood,
and *caṇḍālas*, those men who take the flesh of dogs for food.

19) The liberated soul who recognizes the Supreme
is not a common person of the temporal regime.
Such souls are always firmly fixed in equanimity
and gain Brahman and knowledge of the spirit endlessly.

20) The soul who neither dances when advantage comes his way,
nor, when unwanted things occur, lies down and cries away,
who knows the truth with clarity and lives a saint's routine,
forever is a soul who is absorbed in the Supreme.

21) Enlightened souls do not take pleasure from external senses.
They're satisfied with service as their inner joy commences.
They link with the Supreme and think of Him with concentration,
engrossed in lasting happiness that has no limitation.

22) A learned person knows pursuit of sensual delight
will only lead directly to a miserable plight.
Attaching to a pleasure that begins and soon is through
is something the intelligent and learned never do.

23) By practicing a tolerant approach to sense desire
and mastering the six demands before their flesh expires,

a man or woman celebrates a triumph all around
while others simply cry or die, collapsing to the ground.

24) By giving up externals and embracing joy within,
enlightened souls who roam this world devoid of selfish whims
gain freedom in pursuance of the Absolute regime,
abandoning illusion and attaining the Supreme.

25) A sage creates no sin by helping other people out.
Supremely liberated, he is freed from any doubts.

26) Those souls released from lust and anger, learned and persistent,
extremely serious, realized and properly judicious,
shall overcome the influence of nature's energies
and reach the Absolute, where they remain perpetually.

27, 28) Now hear as I describe the eight-fold mystic yogic way
that takes the yogi far beyond the modes of nature's sway.
While active hearing, touching, smelling, tasting things, or viewing,
a yogi stays unmoved within, no matter what he's doing.
With inner vision focused on a third, internal eye,
while keeping breaths within the nostrils softly minimized,
and focusing the eyes upon the ending of the nose,
the transcendental yogi remains steady and composed.
Such yogis reach a higher state, their spiritual ideal,
released from any urges, fear or anger they may feel.

29) The soul who understands Me well as mysticism's best
has everything he needs to rise to spiritual success.
By knowing I control the worlds, the gods and all that be,
that sacrifice, austerity and work are meant for Me,
and that I am the friend of all, indeed the very best—
though in a troubled world, you will be peaceful, nonetheless.

Bhaktivedanta Swami thus recites śrī-gītār gān
to please the pure devotees always rapt in Krishna's song.

Thus ends the fifth chapter of Śrimad Bhagavad-gītā *named*
karma-sannyāsa-yoga *or action in Kṛṣṇa consciousness.*

Chapter 6

Practice in the State of Transcendence

(Dhyāna-yoga)

1) *Lord Krishna said*:
The true mystic renunciate sets fruits of work aside
and not the work itself, as lesser mystics may prescribe.
Though workers with attachment chase illusory pursuits,
to merely give up work falls short of giving up its fruits.

2) The external renunciate with internal desires
finds he cannot reach yoga while his senses are on fire.

3) So neophytes in yoga hone their duties to progress,
while practiced yogis, one by one, give up external quests.

4) By giving up all sensual, material desires,
one comes to the renunciation for which one aspires.
The scriptures say such yogis have a sheltered situation,
becoming elevated on the path of liberation.[18]

5) By working with detachment and resolve, one saves the soul
from endless wells of worldliness, where it has long been pulled.
A friendship with the mind makes this much easier to do,
for otherwise the mind is like Hiranyakasipu.[XVIII]

6) A person who controls the mind secures the best of friends,
while one who cannot do so has an enemy within.

18 Arjuna proposes to renounce the fight. Krishna says that to be truly renounced he should fight without attachment to the results and gradually give up all material desires. That state is actual yoga, or connection with the Supreme.

7) The masters of the mind achieve the greatest victory,
for they approach the Supersoul and know tranquility.
Regardless if they're cold or hot, hold infamy or fame
or happiness or misery, their outlook is the same.

8) Content in mind through knowledge and ensuing realization,
immersed in spirit, self-controlled in every situation,
such transcendental mystics know to always stay aloof.
Both gold and pebbles look the same to those who know the truth.

9) A transcendental yogi can regard impartially
a cherished friend, a stranger, and an outright enemy.
Yes, those of greater wisdom can see people of all kinds,
the saints, the sinners, everybody, with an equal mind.[19]

10) A yogi in a private place, detached and worry-free,
has neither wants nor any sense of false propriety.
He always keeps his mind controlled and spends most of his time
transcendent in renunciation, rapt in the Divine.

11-12) While sitting on a deerskin cloth set neither low nor high,
a yogi seeks to reach transcendence, growing purified.
By focusing the mind and senses, yogis learn the art
of rooting out impurities, uncluttering the heart.

13-14) Maintaining body, neck, and head in straight, unmoving pose,
absorbed and sober, focused on the ending of the nose,

19 Krishna next explains the first stages of traditional yoga practice.

with mind subdued, devoid of fear and intimate relations,
a yogi thinks of Me alone in perfect meditation.

15) Persistent yoga practice brings a transcendental state
in which the body, mind and spirit all cooperate.
Such yogis gain the nectar of material cessation
which leads to My abode of endless peace and celebration.

16) But yogis can't be yogis if they fast or if they're stuffed
or if they sleep too much or if they do not sleep enough.

17) With regulated eating, sleeping, waking, work and play,
the practiced yogi rises to the transcendental plane.

18) Released from sense desires through his mental discipline,
a yogi stays aloof, content with happiness within.

19) As lamps in windless caves produce an unremitting flame,
a first-class yogi meditates with faith that doesn't change.

20-23) A yogi's mind is pure and fixed in spiritual pursuits.
His perfect abstinence from sense enjoyment is the proof.
To seek the truth beyond the senses fills the heart with bliss,
with mind content to see the self in perfect consciousness.
No other happiness appeals, no tragedy can shake
a yogi from absorption in this perfect mystic state.

24) Enthusiastic, patient yogis, freed from all possessions,
achieve a transcendental state and come to full perfection.
Their minds and senses pacified in perfect regulation,
they feel contrite and end the plight of mental speculation.

25) As step by step the yogi shuns the pleasures of the senses,
exclusive mental focus on the inner self commences.

26) Because the mind is so unsteady, shaky, and averse,
it wanders unabated all throughout the universe.
A yogi learns to regulate and purify the mind
by keeping it subordinate to spirit all the time.

27) With minds absorbed and peaceful, yogis feel great ecstasy.
Their former carnal, karmic passions yield to purity.
The mode of goodness dominant, their sinful acts redeemed,
identified with spirit, yogis relish the Supreme.

28) The joyous yogis, freed from sin and all contamination,
can step by step connect with the Supreme in fascination.
Absorbed and transcendental, yogis shed the lower modes
and pure, unfiltered vision of Brahman, the spirit, grows.
On having come in touch with the Supreme within themselves,
such yogis come to witness Him in everybody else.

29) Endowed with equal vision, realized yogis clearly see
the all-pervading Supersoul in every entity.

30) The yogi, seeing Me in all things animate or still,
alone transcends the influence of things material.
Such persons, My devotees, come to know and share with Me
affectionate exchanges beyond dry philosophy.

31) Aware that I am in the heart of everyone he sees,
aware I am existing everywhere that he may be,
consistent in whatever circumstances he may find,
a yogi worships Me with service, keeping Me in mind.

32) Accepting friends and strangers with an equal attitude,
a perfect yogi welcomes all with non-judgmental mood.
He won't impose on others his content or sad condition.
Such persons are known everywhere as souls of equal vision.[20]

33) *Arjuna said*:
O Krishna, Madhusūdana,[XIX] this system you've explained,
designed for realization on the transcendental plane,
appears to be entirely impossible for me.
My mind is so unsteady that it changes constantly.

34) O Krishna, do You really think a yogi can prevail?
The mind is so robust that one seems guaranteed to fail.
The agitated, stubborn mind refuses to give in.
To manage it seems harder than to supervise the wind.

---

20 On hearing of this strict yogic discipline and its sublime results, Arjuna now asks questions that naturally come to everyone's mind.

35) *Lord Krishna said*:
O mighty son of Kunti, yes, the restless mind is stout,
and conquering the mind is very hard, without a doubt.
And yet if your mundane pursuits turn spiritual instead,
by practicing detachment, you will soon come out ahead.

36) Although it can be difficult to check the mind's demands,
it nonetheless is possible for one who understands.
By taking My detailed advice and trying cent per cent,
one gains self-realization and perfects what he attempts.

37) *Arjuna said*:
O Krishna, what becomes of yogis striving for perfection
who deviate and later choose a more mundane direction?

38) Distracted from the spiritual success that they had sought,
bewildered yogis also fail in this world, do they not?
Do they become some riven clouds the winds can push about?
O mighty-armed Lord Krishna, help me pierce and shed this doubt.

39) My dear Lord Krishna, since You know all things that can be known,
such doubts about my future can be solved by You alone.

40) *Lord Krishna said*:
O Pārtha, listen now about the fallen yogi's fate,
for endless dangers in this world face every candidate.
A yogi is protected, both in this life or the next,
for acting in auspiciousness will always bring success.

41) Should yogis fall, their piety still brings them godly bliss,
for they are born in wealthy homes, or those of righteousness.

42) Or sometimes fallen yogis reappear in their next life
as children of a learned, transcendental man and wife.
Though such a birth is rare indeed, the soul who so appears
remains with saintly people and has nothing more to fear.

43) O son of Kuru, such a fallen yogi then revives
the consciousness accumulated in his former lives.
With fresh intelligence, determined yogis then progress
and carry on their practice to their ultimate success.

44) By nature, reborn yogis come to eagerly explore
the transcendental practices a yogi must perform.
Inquisitive to link with the Supreme, such yogis spurn
the formal Vedic rites that bring material returns.

45) By practicing for many lives such yogis then proceed
to cross the sea of misery and perfectly succeed.

46) Rich men cannot touch a yogi,
wise men cannot touch a yogi,
nor can those whose lives are quite austere.
Therefore, O Arjuna, you
should be a worthy yogi too
in every time and place and atmosphere.

47) And of all types of yogis, scriptures certify as best
the one who always links with Me in thoughtful consciousness.
Such faithful yogis render loving service unto Me.
Arjuna, know such yogis are superior indeed.[21]

Bhaktivedanta Swami thus recites śrī-gītār gān
to please the pure devotees always rapt in Krishna's song.

Thus ends the sixth chapter of Śrimad Bhagavad-gītā *named*
abhyāsa-yoga *or practice in the state of transcendence.*

21 Just as He has done with *karma yoga* (detached work) and *jñāna yoga* (cultivation of knowledge), after describing *dhyana yoga* (mystic, meditative yoga) in this chapter, Krishna circles back to *bhakti yoga* (personal service to Krishna in devotion) as the ultimate path. The next six chapters of *Bhagavad-gītā* focus on *bhakti yoga.*

Chapter 7

Knowledge of the Absolute

(vijñāna-yoga)

1) *Lord Krishna said:*
O Pārtha, thus far you have heard how yoga is the means
to shed your doubts, find shelter and become attached to Me.
Now listen and learn more how bhakti yoga purifies.
When rendered in pure goodness, bhakti fully satisfies.

2) Just hear from Me attentively the truth that corresponds
to both the finite and the infinite that lies beyond.
By mastering this comprehensive knowledge, you will see
how easily you can resolve transcendent mysteries.

3) Of many thousand people, hardly one seeks out the truth.
Of many seekers, hardly one attains the Absolute.
Though diligent and qualified, of them few are astute
enough to see reality and fathom Me in truth. [22]

4) My separated energies of matter are eight kinds:
Earth and water, air and fire, ego, and the mind,
along with ether (emptiness) and all intelligence.
These eight are My inferior, external opulence.

5) O mighty-armed Arjuna, far beyond these lesser eight
is spirit, My expansive might of vastly greater weight.
This spirit is the living force, the tiny spirit souls
who try to exploit matter and believe they're in control.

---

22 *Bhakti yoga* means devotional service rendered in love, and to love someone, we must know who they are. Thus at this point Krishna explains Himself more fully to Arjuna.

6) Material and spiritual—these twofold potencies
combine to form all species known as living entities.
Because I am the source of these divergent energies
the universe arises from and comes to end in Me.

7) Of every truth of every kind, O conqueror of wealth,
there is no truth that passes Me or lies beyond Myself.
Because the very universe resides in Me, it's said
that everything depends on Me as pearls are strung on thread.

8) I am the satisfying taste of water, Kuntī's son.
I am the light originating from the moon and sun.
Of all the Vedic letters I am A-U-M, the best,
as well as every letter-sound produced by all the rest.

9) I am the fragrance of the earth, the power of the sun,
the life of all that lives, the penance every sage has done.

10) Of everything that lives I am the fundamental seed.
I am the truth eternally, and all observe My lead.
O Pārtha, as the Supersoul I live in every heart,
supplying power to the mighty, wisdom to the smart.

11) O best among the Bhāratas, please understand that I
am known by many glories I shall briefly now describe.
Among strong leaders I am strength, yet I've no greed or lust.
The procreative act is Me, when scriptural and just.

12) The good, the dark, the passionate, three modes of nature's sway
arise from Me yet never bother Me in any way.

13) Throughout this world, illusion from these three modes is the norm,
preventing all from knowing My supreme and endless form.

14) These modes, My outward energy, are hard to overcome,
yet one who shelters at My feet will find their grip succumb.[23]

15) The modes' influence generates four kinds of godless men:
the grossly foolish, those who use their intellect to sin,
those men who think themselves quite wise but don't know who they are,
and demons who believe the goal of life is waging war.

16) Four types of pious souls include those people in distress,
the needy, the inquisitive who put Me to the test,
and learned seekers. All four turn devotedly to Me,
avoiding this life's useless wars and vile mentalities.

17) Among these four, the wise and learned seeker stands apart,
for this beloved soul serves Me with strong and sturdy heart.

18) All four types are magnanimous and doubtlessly achieve
consistent, steady progress to the highest purity.

---

23 Krishna now describes how the modes of nature, His material energy, influence everyone to be in various relationships with Him. Less intelligent, arrogant, and wicked people reject Krishna, while wise and humble people approach Him, even if only out of curiosity or distress.

And yet the learned seeker links most thoroughly with Me
and through outstanding knowledge gains the highest destiny.

19) Through many lifetimes, step by step, the seekers' scope expands
till gradually their virtue lets them fully understand
that every quest for knowledge ends at Vāsudeva's feet.
The scriptures say such great, exalted souls are rare indeed.[24]

20) As long as one's desires in this mundane world persist,
surrender and attachment unto Me will not exist.
In fact, a person caught in some material pursuit
gives worship to demigods and not the Absolute.

21) As Supersoul, I'm in the hearts of such distracted souls.
Although their lesser worship only leads to lesser goals,
by worshiping the demigods, their newly steady faith
will soon become an asset leading to a higher place.

22) Endowed with faith, such people worship demigods for wealth,
not knowing that their benefits have all come from Myself.
Since everything their worship brings elapses in due time,
their motivated service is a futile paradigm.

23) To fleeting planets of the gods do their devotees go,
but My devotees settle in My Absolute abode.

---

24 Krishna now concludes this chapter describing impersonalism and demigod worship, two spiritually related goals that are nonetheless subordinate to *bhakti*.

24) To those still less intelligent, Brahman is the supreme,
that undivided changeless light pervading everything.
Such people never see My form or personality
that sages know as endless, wise, and full of ecstasy.
I am just like the sun, forever giving life itself.
Though others cannot see Me, I'm complete within Myself.

25) Since foolish people cannot see Me, they can never know
that I am inexhaustible, the unborn Supersoul.

26) Arjuna, in My endless, blissful form I clearly see
the present, past and future, yet these fools can't fathom Me.
They cannot see that everything is under My control,
nor can they see how I know everything there is to know.

27) These most unlucky people sink into dualities
as hatred and desire spawn their false realities.
O son of Bharat, from their very birth they are harassed
by prejudices binding them from many lifetimes past.

28) But those who stop all sinful acts and take up pious deeds
release themselves from servitude to false dualities.
By serving Me with fortitude that never can be swayed,
they live in this unstable world completely unafraid.

29) Accepting shelter in this world by serving Me, the wise
pursue the path of freedom from senescence and demise.

By grasping the impersonal and Supersoul as well,
such yogis know all wisdom transcendentalists may tell.

30) Aware of Me as governing all gods, all sacrifice,
and all within the universe itself, the very wise
connect with Me as Supersoul. And when their bodies die,
they go at once to My abode, forever to reside.

Bhaktivedanta Swami thus recites śrī-gītār gān
to please the pure devotees always rapt in Krishna's song.

Thus ends the seventh chapter of Śrimad Bhagavad-gītā *named* vijñana-yoga *or Knowledge of the Absolute.*

Chapter 8

Attaining the Supreme

(akṣarabrahma-yoga)

1,2) *Arjuna said*:
O Krishna, please explain Brahman, the self and selfish deeds.
And what about the demigods—what do they oversee?
O killer of the Madhu demon, who rules sacrifice?
And how can I remember you when I give up my life?

3) *Lord Krishna said*:
The permanent and subtle living beings are Brahman.
Among all beings, I'm Supreme, and known as *Bhagavān.*
Full knowledge means to know Brahman, the Supersoul and Me
as *Bhagavān*, or Godhead's greatest Personality.
The selfish actions of the souls produce their outer forms.
All this is knowledge absolute. Now listen, there is more.

4) The demigods are part of My vast Universal form,
as is the sum of matter as it constantly transforms.
Regarding sacrifice, as God, it's only meant for Me,
for I sit in the heart of every living entity.

5) When death, therefore, obliges souls in bodies to move out,
if one remembers Me, he gains My nature without doubt.

6) Whatever state of life that one recalls when death prevails
will manifest again in one's next lifetime without fail.

7) So always turn your body, mind, and intellect to Me.
Surrender, and attainment of Myself is guaranteed.

8) To come to Me at death is easy with a fixed routine
of thinking of Me always as the Personal Supreme.

9) Now hear how to remember Me,
the Person who knows everything,
forever in control of all that be.
Unseen by mundane observation,
subtly I hold creation,
bright and blissful, doing as I please.

10) As he expires, the faithful soul
who made Me his exclusive goal,
his life air focused in between his brows,
achieves the transcendental state,
his pure devotion unabated,
reaching Me as he concludes his vows.[25]

11) Now listen to yet more details
about the sages who prevail
in living as the Vedic texts condone.
They undertake a life aloof
from mundane commonplace pursuits
and live as celibates while chanting oṁ.

25 In reply to Arjuna's questions, Krishna, as God, has further explained Himself and how to think of Him. Such self-descriptive passages throughout *Bhagavad-gītā* make the book unique. Other Vedic texts glorify subordinate demigods, but no demigods proclaim themselves supreme. And although the Abrahamic scriptures glorify God, rarely in them does God reveal much about Himself. Only in *Bhagavad-gītā* do we find God giving detailed and thorough descriptions of both Himself and various relationships with Him.

12) Securing gateways to the senses
and all outer circumstances,
life airs all converged on the third eye,
with mind in heartfelt meditation's
transcendental situation,
yogis grow completely qualified.

13) By chanting *oṁ*, the absolute
and revered syllable of truth,
remembering Me as one's body dies,
one comes to the Vaikuṇṭha[XX] life
in worlds where Śrī Hari[XXI] resides
and at His feet is ever glorified.

14) The yogis never deviate
for I am all they contemplate.
O Pārtha, they are steadfast in their aim.
So resolute and self-controlled,
the yogis serve with heart and soul
and find Me very easy to attain.

15) Such great souls leave this fleeting, painful world and don't return.
Attaining Me, there's no perfection left for them to earn.

16) Within the fourteen worlds, including even upper tiers,
where Lord Brahmā[XXII] has domiciled for many, many years,
one's life is still ephemeral. The souls come out and in.
But one who shelters in My service won't take birth again.

17) Four billion human years comprise Lord Brahmā's single day.
A thousand yuga cycles—and his night is just the same.

18) In these three worlds, at Brahmā's dawn, the souls take mortal dress,
and at his dusk they reassume a state unmanifest.

19) These helpless souls of every type are born with every dawn.
Again and yet again, their mortal bodies are withdrawn.

20) Above all mortal planets lies the spiritual abode
where time does not exist to vanquish, alter, or corrode.
And while the force of time destroys all things in this domain,
in that sublime abode one's blissful life remains unchanged.

21) I always stay in that abode of endless, perfect form,
and others coming there as well remain forevermore.

22) Though stationed there, as Supersoul I nonetheless pervade
all aspects of creation that could ever be surveyed.
O Pārtha, My undeviating servant thus can tell
that I as Supersoul reside within the heart as well.

23) Great scion of the Bhāratas,[XXIII] now hear as I explain
how at the time of death the yogi reaches higher planes.

24) The knowers of Brahman who leave this world in times of light,
at certain sacred moments, with the sun in northern flight,

will rise to that Supreme abode. This is, at least, the view
of those who like to speculate or work for karmic fruits.

25) But one who dies in smoky skies or nights of waning moon
or when the sun is in the south cannot achieve such boons.
They may attain the moon planet, above this lowly Earth,
but failing to achieve Brahman, they take another birth.

26) To die in dark or die in light, as Vedic scriptures state,
determines whether one is freed or must reincarnate.

27) Although My servants understand these two divergent paths,
they never grow bewildered by this lifetime's aftermath.
They stay within My shelter as persistent devotees.
So therefore, son of Pṛthā, always fix your mind on Me.

28) Some like to follow Vedic scriptures,
sacrifice and all its strictures,
penances or lavish charity.
Though each path has its advocates,
all types of pious benefits
and more accrue to Krishna's devotee.

Bhaktivedanta Swami thus recites śrī-gītār gān
to please the pure devotees always rapt in Krishna's song.

Thus ends the eighth chapter of Śrimad Bhagavad-gītā *named*
akṣarabrahma-yoga *or attaining the supreme.*

Chapter 9

The Most Confidential Knowledge

(rājaguhya-yoga)

1) *Lord Krishna said:*
My dear Arjuna, since you're never envious of Me,
I'll speak more confidential knowledge. Listen carefully,
for you will benefit by what I'm just about to say,
the wisdom to drive worldly inauspiciousness away.

2) Among all education, this instruction is the king,
with topics far more intimate than any you might glean.
These pure and deathless lessons have the power to transform.
Surpassing all religion, they are joyfully performed.

3) The faithless soul upon this path, O killer of the foe,
will only find futility in all they say and know.
Austere as they may be, they never shall attain to Me,
remaining on the path of birth and death in misery.

4) In My unmanifest and formless feature I pervade
the universe itself and all from which it has been made.
Although the universe retains its origins in Me,
I always stay aloof from My own cosmic energies.

5) Such separation from My own creation does demand
tremendous mystic power, inconceivable to man.
From that position I maintain all living entities
who vacillate between mundane and sacred potencies.

6) As winds exist and swirl within the all-pervading sky,
these living beings come from Me, and in Me they reside.

7) In time the universe of matter comes upon its end
and then returns to Me to be created once again.
Unmanifest or manifest, in portion or in whole,
creation, say My followers, is under My control.

8) And as My potent nature thus repeatedly creates,
I also oversee how living beings operate.

9) O Dhanañjaya, you must know that I am never bound
by these creations and destructions cycling round and round.
For Me, none of these various transactions are like chores,
for I remain indifferent, today, and evermore.

10) I easily turn matter into live, organic things
in shapes including mobile and immobile living beings.
The endless birth and death of great or tiny entities
are simply transformations of My varied energies.

11) Unable to acknowledge how My energies perform,
the less intelligent deride Me in My human form.
Though everything belongs to Me, such fools can never see
how I remain the transcendental Lord of all that be.

12) While chasing after wealth or ordinary education,
those people who disparage Me can't fill their expectations.
Such atheists and demons leave Me, choosing to misuse
their precious human life engaged in sensual pursuits.

Bewildered by material existence, they cannot
escape the beatings of illusion in which they are caught.

13) The great souls, on the other hand, have purified their minds
and turn for shelter to devotion, serving the Divine.
Associating with sincere devotees, they can see
that I alone originate all living entities.

14) These great souls have great qualities derived from praising Me,
surrendering each word, each worship, each activity.
They're always chanting, always serving, always resolute.
Become like them and realize Me, the ultimate pursuit.

15) Now, impure persons worship Me in three less learned ways:
the worship of oneself as all, with none in second place,
the worship of the countless universal demigods,
and worship of a formless, vast impersonal façade.

16, 17) But it is I who am the rite of sacrifice to gods.
I am the chant, the offering, the healing herbal balms.
I am the fire, gifts, and ghee that sacrifice demands.
I am the parents and the gods on whom creation stands.
I am the learned grandfather, the purifying *oṁ*,
and I am all the *Ṛg*, *Yajur* and *Sāma* Vedic tomes.

18, 19) I am the witness, refuge, and sustainer of all beings.
I am the goal, the origin and ending of all things.
I am the endless seed, the One who fashions and maintains.

I am both death and life that comes when clouds provide the rains.
And I am immortality. Arjuna, do you see
how all things made of matter and of spirit live in Me?

20) All those who use the Vedic texts
for pleasure this life and the next
will find their sacrifice for Me askew.
Through cleansing sins, this pious gambit
brings them birth on Indra's planet
joining gods to drink the soma juice.

21) Though heaven's pleasures cover pain,
one's pious karma slowly drains
and with it goes the godly reveling.
And thus, the Vedic sense enjoyment
really is a glass of poison.
Further birth and death are all it brings.

22) But others, who instead consider Me exclusively,
absorbed as My devotees, their minds dwelling upon Me,
receive from Me whatever happiness they may desire
for I maintain what they possess and give what they require.

23) The faith of those who worship other gods is meant for Me,
though offered up in lieu of true religiosity.

24) For every sacrifice is really meant for Me alone,
and one who sees this understands all knowledge to be known.

But those who separate from Me and worship someone else
just end up feeling more and more bewildered in themselves.

25) On those who worship demigods, the heavens are bestowed.
All those who worship ancestors proceed to their abodes.
All those who worship ghosts and spirits join them, guaranteed,
but those who worship Me are satisfied and come to Me.
Because I share with everyone My opulence galore,
My worship is quite easy, even for the very poor.

26) Some leaves or flowers, fruits, or water, set with care for Me,
and offered in devotion, I accept most willingly.
Yes, those who offer little things with loving, kind emotion
will satisfy Me fully by the shine of their devotion.

27) Because you're fixed as My dear servant, everything you do
is offered in devotion with a sweet and serving mood.
So sacrifices that you make, each morsel that you eat,
and every austerity, just offer unto Me.

28) In this way you are free from the results of what you do.
Reactions, inauspicious or auspicious, don't accrue,
for serving Me is yoga in complete renunciation.
Absorb your mind in Me and I shall be your destination.

29) I see each living entity with equal disposition.
I do not favor or disfavor anyone's condition.

And yet whoever renders loving service unto Me
remains with Me, for I return the same affinity.

30) At times a person offers Me undeviating service,
yet later somehow causes some detestable disturbance.
When he resumes his normal service with determination,
he once again is saintly in his proper situation.

31) His righteousness restored, this errant servant shall improve,
and very soon the guilt he feels is thoroughly removed.
Arjuna, son of Kunti, hear My firm and endless vow:
destruction of My devotee I never shall allow.

32) Attaining shelter in Me, even those of lower birth—
the merchants, workers, prostitutes, the meat-eaters and worse—
shall all have My protection and eventually proceed
to My abode, Vaikuṇṭha, where their bliss is guaranteed.

33) And what to speak of pious *brāḥmaṇas*, steeped in sacred texts?
And what to speak of righteous *kṣatriyas*, those who protect?
Though also born into this fleeting world of misery,
they too can practice loving service, ever worry-free.

34) Become My pure devotee and absorb your mind in Me.
Engage yourself in serving Me with love incessantly.
Bow down to Me in worship and by such activity,
your practice of devotion leads directly unto Me.

Bhaktivedānta Swāmi thus recites śrī-gītār gān
to please the pure devotees always rapt in Krishna's song.

Thus ends the ninth chapter of Śrimad Bhagavad-gītā *named* rājaguhya-yoga, *the most confidential knowledge.*

Chapter 10

The Opulence of the Absolute

(vibhūti-yoga)

1) *Lord Krishna said*:
Now hear these words that build auspicious fortune even more,
this knowledge absolute, surpassing all I've said before.

2) The sages and the demigods can't grasp My opulence,
for I preceded all of them, and from Me they commence.
Regardless how one speculates or muses without end,
how much of Me could anybody truly comprehend?

3) Discerning that I am Supreme, with no beginning date,
the blissful, ageless, changeless, all-perceiving Potentate,
one vanquishes reactions from all sins of any depth
and lives without delusion even in this world of death.

4,5) Intelligence, determination, kindness, honesty,
mastery of the senses and the mind, austerity,
cheerfulness, dejection, confidence, anxiety,
birth and death, contentedness, both fame and infamy,
peacefulness, nonviolence, and equanimity;
the wise know well I am the source of all these qualities.

6) Such sages as Marici, seven saints and many others,
including the Kumaras, Sanaka and his three brothers,
and all the fourteen Manus, the forefathers of mankind
who populate the planets are, in fact, born of My mind.

7) On seeing who I am, My strength and mystic opulence,
a soul becomes a yogi and is thoroughly convinced

that serving Me devotedly reveals the highest truth
that leads, in turn, to unalloyed devotional pursuits.[26]

8) The worlds of flesh and spirit both originate from Me.
The wise will therefore give their hearts and serve Me earnestly.
While ordinary, mundane people do not know this truth,
the truly learned understand that I am absolute.

9) My pure devotees always think of Me within themselves.
They dedicate their very lives to Me and no one else.
Discussing My eternal pastimes satisfies their minds
and helps them stay absorbed in blissful service all the time.

10) For those absorbed in faithful, loving service I bestow
the knowledge, strength, and wisdom to return to My abode.

11) For My determined servants who set mundane goals aside,
I bring the lamp of knowledge to their hearts from deep inside.
As lightning flashes drive away the darkness from the skies,
I burn away their ignorance and help them become wise.

12, 13) *Arjuna said*:
O Krishna, You're the purest and the greatest, highest truth.
You are the ultimate abode, Your shelter absolute.
As the unborn, unprecedented Personality,

26 The following four verses are known as the four summary verses (*chatuḥ-ślokī*) of the *Bhagavad-gītā*. These well-known texts describe how the soul and God interact. After hearing them, Arjuna declares his devotion for his friend Krishna, now also his Deity. Then Arjuna asks a very pertinent question.

Your transcendental form is the Supreme authority.
Devarṣi Nārada, Asita, Vyās and all great sages
recite these truths about You, both today and through the ages.

14) O killer of the Keshi demon, everything You've said
exactly matches all the Vedic wisdom I have read.
Ananta Śeṣa's[XXIV] countless mouths can't praise You properly,
and neither gods nor demons know Your personality.

15) Yes, only You can know Yourself, for every other being
originates from You alone, the Source of everything.
O God of gods, O Lord of all, be kind now and unveil
Your endless, mystic opulence in even more detail.

16) Your opulence allows You to pervade the fourteen worlds,
maintaining for you everywhere the fame You so deserve.

17) O greatest of all yogis, kindly tell me if You please,
how I can meditate on Your unbounded qualities.
Your nature and Your opulence are limitless and grand.
In what ways, by Your mercy, can I somewhat understand?

18) O Krishna, O Janārdana, I'm keen to hear You say
some words about the many opulences You display.
And even if I heard this nectar time and time again
I still would not be satisfied or wish that it would end.

19) *Lord Krishna said:*

O best among the Kurus, since you ask, I shall explain
some aspects of the endless opulences I maintain.
Now give your mind to hearing traits that I consider most
outstanding and descriptive of My own unrivaled post.

20) O Guḍākeśa[XXV], I protect each living entity.
Their origin, existence and conclusion come from Me.

21) I'm Viṣṇu of Ādityas and the sun among all lights.
Of Maruts I'm Marici and of stars, the moon at night.

22) Of Vedas I'm the Sama and of gods, Indra, the king.
Of senses I'm the mind, the central force in living beings.

23) I'm Śiva of the Rudras and of Yakṣas I'm Kuvera.
I'm Agni of the Vasus and of mountains I'm Sumeru.

24) Of chiefs I'm Kārtikeya and of priests, Bṛhaṣpati.
Of reservoirs of water, I'm the vast, enormous sea.

25) Among the greatest sages, Bhṛgu Muni is like Me.
Of syllables, the sound of oṁ presents Me perfectly.
Of sacrifices, *japa*[XXVI] is the one I most approve,
and I'm the Himālayas among things that can't be moved.

26) Among all trees I am the banyan, massive in its size.
Among all godly sages, I am Nārada, the wise.

Among all the Gandharvas, I am Citrarath, their king.
I am the sage Kapila, most refined of perfect beings.

27) Among all horses I am Uccaiḥśravā, who arose
when gods and demons churned the sea of milk in My abode.
Among all elephants I am Airāvata, the best.
Among all men I am the monarch, ruler of the rest.

28, 29) Of weapons I'm the thunderbolt, the mightiest of blows.
Of cows I am Surabhi who gives milk in endless flow.
Of causes of conception, I am Cupid, god of love.
Of snakes I'm Vāsuki and Śesh, with many hoods above.
Of sea life I'm Varuna, Aryamā among forebears,
and I am Yamarāj, bestowing justice everywhere.

30) Of demons I'm Prahlād, the one who thirsts for pure devotion.
Of factors I am time, for it subdues all other notions.
I am the lion, of all beasts the undisputed king.
I am Garuḍa, best of birds, with Vishnu on his wings.

31) Of things that move I am the wind, by far the mightiest.
Of carriers of weapons, I'm Paraśurām, the best.
Among aquatics I'm the shark, unmatched in his domain.
Among all flowing rivers, Mother Ganga is My name.

32) Arjuna, how My varied, boundless opulence extends!
I start and maintain everything and cause all things to end.

Among all kinds of knowledge, I am knowledge of the self.
Among all kinds of truth, I am conclusive truth itself.

33) Among all letters I am "A." Of compound words, you see,
I am the dual compound, though I've no duality.
I am Brahmā of all who build and time of what destroys.
As Rudra, My great power of destruction is deployed.

34) Though I am death, the end of all, devouring all resistance,
I also generate all things that come into existence.
Of women, I'm the beautiful and steadfast qualities
of fortune, wisdom, patience, language, fame, and memory.

35) Among the Vedic hymns I am the Bṛhat-sāma lines.
Of poems I am Gāyatrī, the best and most sublime.
Of seasons you may know I am the flower-bearing spring.
Of months I am November, time of peace and harvesting.

36) I'm victory among attempts, the splendor of the splendid,
and gambling of deceptions meant to cheat the ill-intended.
I'm enterprise, adventure, and the strength among the strong.
Descriptions of My opulence continue on and on.

37) Of sages I am Vyāsadev, who wrote the Vedic truths.
Of Vṛṣṇis I am Vāsudev. Of Pāṇḍavās, I'm you.
Of humans I'm the Āryan, the most cultured type of man,
and I am Śukrācārya among those who think and plan.

38) I am the rod of punishment among administrators.
I am the proper judgment of judicial arbitrators.
Of secrets I'm the silence that is always necessary.
I am the wisdom of the wise. All else is secondary.

39) My dear Arjuna, I'm the seed of everything that be.
Both moving and non-moving beings perish without Me.

40) Although I have described to you My opulence in brief,
O conqueror of enemies, My glories never cease.

41) So, any opulence you see, including strength or wealth,
have all been manifested out of mercy from Myself.
A spark of My resplendence generates all that exists,
and you can feel Me everywhere by understanding this.

42) Arjuna, what more can I say than all I now have shared?
Wherever any strength exists, I'm situated there.
Through massive universes, My one fragment permeates.
In deep and dark illusion, My one spark illuminates.

Bhaktivedanta Swami thus recites śrī-gītār gān
to please the pure devotees always rapt in Krishna's song.

Thus ends the tenth chapter of Śrimad Bhagavad-gītā *named* vibhūti-yoga, *the opulence of the absolute.*

Chapter 11

The Universal Form

(viśwarūpa-darśana-yoga)

1) *Arjuna said*:
On hearing these profound instructions given by Your grace,
illusion is undone with only truth left in its place.
This spiritual and confidential truth has now dismissed
the many doubts and questions that have plagued my consciousness.

2) I now have heard from You details of two eternal truths,
both how creation happens and of how it all concludes.
Creation is extensive, yet Your endless forms comprise
the best of it, Supreme controller, Lord of lotus eyes.

3) O greatest of all persons, if You think me qualified,
I now would like to see and know You from another side.

4) O master of all mystics, if You think my eyes of worth,
reveal to me Your endless form that spans the universe.[27]

5) *Lord Krishna said*:
O son of Pṛthā, just behold this overwhelming swarm
of hundreds and then thousands of divine, transcendent forms.
Just see the great variety of multi-colored shades
adorning My expansions in this mystical display.

6) Behold the Vasus, Rudras, Aśvini-kumārs and more.
Behold the wondrous, awesome gods as none have seen before.

---

27 Although Arjuna now accepts Krishna as God, he still seeks a glimpse of Krishna's all-powerful, all-pervading presence in the visible universe. When Krishna complies, Arjuna has an abrupt and unexpected change of attitude towards his friend.

7) Now everything existing is before you to survey,
both moving and non-moving, transcendental and mundane.
O conqueror of sleep, as Krishna, I am absolute.
Observe My glories carefully. There is no higher truth.

8) You are My pure devotee and yet still you cannot see
My full immense, gigantic form of cosmic majesty.
So now the gift of eyes divine on you I shall bestow
so that you can experience directly all I show.[28]

9) *Sañjaya said:*
Now hear, King Dhṛtarāṣṭra, what Arjuna then could see
when Lord Krishna displayed His hidden, vast reality.

10, 11) Arjuna witnessed countless eyes that flashed like lightning strikes
in countless bodies bearing gems of rare, celestial types.
He saw celestial weapons too, and garlands of fine taste
adorning every form along with scents and sandal paste.

12) If one could see a million suns arising at one time,
one might attain an inkling of the vast, unending shine
the Universal Form displayed upon appearing there.
For otherwise, what evidence, what brilliance could compare?

---

28 Sañjaya, the narrator of the *Bhagavad-gītā*, speaks directly in this chapter, his only appearance other than at the beginning and end of the text.

13) And then Arjuna saw the endless portions of creation
contained in Krishna's body, each in proper situation.
Divided one by one, and yet conjoined exactly right,
each one shone brightly with a natural effulgent light.

14) Bewildered and amazed, Arjuna, hair standing on end,
then bowed his head and joined his palms to venerate his friend.
Before this godly gathering, his safety a concern,
Arjuna felt unsettled and began to pray, in turn:

15) *Arjuna said:*
Within Your body, opulences
visible before my senses
far exceed what speaking can express.
I now perceive all living beings,
moving and non-moving things,
gigantic in their range and yet compressed.
I see the gods of awesome power,
Brahmā on his lotus flower,
sacred serpents rising all about,
Lord Śiva, saints, detached and smart,
the Supersoul in every heart—
Supreme Controller, no one is left out.

16) Within Your body I can see
so many arms, so many teeth,
so many eyes and bellies without end.
And now I see from where I stand

how everywhere Your form expands.
Almighty Lord, how can I comprehend?

17) Bedecked with crowns of perfect fit
and weapons, clubs, and razor discs,
Your brilliant shine obliterates all gloom.
So radiant that dazzling scene
it makes Your form as hard to see
as staring at the fiery sun at noon.

18) To seek the truth indeed entails
to know You, for you never fail.
You are the final shelter of us all.
O basis of all piety,
O foremost Personality,
You're limitless and inexhaustible.

19) You never start, You never end.
Your unrestricted strength extends
through mighty arms, with sun and moon as eyes.
Your mouths emit such burning flames
the universe is now ablaze.
Your brilliant radiance pervades the skies.

20) Your form expands in every way,
engulfing earth and outer space
and all within, without, or in between.
The lower, mid, and upper worlds

are fearful, awestruck, and disturbed
beholding this great sight they've never seen.

21) The demigods in endless hosts
afraid of You as they come close,
submit to You and pray with folded palms.
The sages, saints, and perfect souls,
well reconciled to Your control,
all pray for peace by singing Vedic psalms.

22) Lord Śiva in his many phases,
Vasus, Maruts, Viśvadevas,
Aśvinī Kumārs and other gods,
the forefathers from Pitriloka,
Gandharvas from Siddhaloka—
all arrive to watch You in great awe.

23) O mighty-armed Lord Krishna, these
respected personalities
become disturbed as You have now appeared.
Your giant form has countless eyes
and mouths and bellies, legs, and thighs.
Your huge, horrific teeth invoke their fear.

24) I see Your omnipresent eyes,
Your countless heads that touch the sky
and hang like streams of blazing, brilliant fire.
To see their multi-colored hues,

has stunned and left me so confused
I've lost the steady mind I so require.

25) To see Your teeth appear like those
of death itself in fiery rows
within Your blazing mouth, leaves me adrift.
I do not know what's good for me.
O Foremost Personality,
please save me from this great apocalypse.

26) Now Dhṛtarāṣṭra's sons, their friends
like Bhīṣma, Droṇa, Karṇa and
the many other soldiers, friend and foe,
I see between Your awful teeth,
entrapped above and underneath,
their bodies smashed and slaughtered, row by row.

27, 28) Enmeshed in Your teeth, everyone
is smashed into oblivion,
inciting visions deep within my mind
of rivers flowing to an ocean,
endless and in constant motion,
seawater and river now combined.

29) These powerful, commanding humans
rushing toward their executions
in Your mouths of all-devouring fire
remind me of a moth who freely

flies into a flame completely,
entering at will its funeral pyre.

30) O Vishnu! How Your mouths are lethal,
all-consuming, burning people,
turning all their lives to history.
It now is clear: no one escapes
Your devastating, scorching rays
that fill the universe with misery.

31) Be merciful, almighty Lord!
Who are You in this awful form?
I bow to You, O Master. Tell me more.
What is the reason You assume
this wondrous form of cosmic doom
no one has ever seen or known before?
Please tell me why this form exists.
Please tell me what Your mission is.
Please tell me why You've come here, I implore.

32) *Lord Krishna said:*
Time I am, the vast assault,
the great devouring death of all.
By My will every planet is destroyed.
As Supersoul who lives within,
I bring all creatures to an end.
I am the force of death no one avoids.
Thus, every warrior gathered here

is guaranteed to disappear
no matter how and where they are deployed.

33) So therefore, fight and win your fame.
This kingdom is now yours to gain.
In joyous battle, kill your enemies.
I say they are already dead
before you even turn your head.
You're just an instrument in what's to be.

34) You see that Bhīṣma, Jayadrath,
with Droṇa, Karṇa, and the lot
of heroes here have already been killed.
So, what need have you to lament,
regardless of your sentiment?
They all have been extinguished by My will.

35) *Sanjaya said*:
On hearing these divine commands
Arjuna stood with folded hands
then prostrated again and yet again.
Now hear, my King, what he said next,
his body shaking, mind perplexed,
with fear and veneration for his friend.

36) *Arjuna said*:
For those who simply grow aware
that You are present everywhere,

with vast, unending majesty and grace,
the world itself becomes sublime.
They madly seek You all the time,
O master of the senses, Hṛṣikesh.
You're thought of so respectfully
and served in all activities
by saintly souls of absolute perfection.
However, those of evil minds,
the demons wickedly inclined,
run off from you in every direction.

37) O Krishna, why do they not seek
the shelter of Your lotus feet
when clearly You're the greatest of the great?
Brahmā himself, the first of beings,
yet serves You as the King of kings,
the Master who initially creates.
Your fame and glories reign supreme,
O endless Lord of everything,
O God of gods, the refuge of all souls.
You are the cause of every cause,
the peerless source of space and stars,
above this world and never known in full.

38) For You are the original,
beyond the mere transitional,
the foremost Personality of God.
If someone could compile a list

of all the matter that exists,
He'd find You are behind the whole façade.
You know all things that can be known.
Our shelter is in You alone.
You're endless, with no limit to be found.
You penetrate and then pervade
this universe that You have made.
By Your unyielding laws are we all bound.

39) You supervise the moon, the air,
the flame, the water everywhere.
You are the very center of each soul.
You are Brahmā, he who creates
the countless species, countless races.
Such is your unrivaled cosmic role.
No other option waits for me
than bowing to Your lotus feet
a thousand times and then a thousand more.
I offer You respects and then
I offer them again, again.
Please place Your glance upon me, my dear Lord.

40) I bow before Your lotus feet
from front and back and in between
O Supersoul of boundless energy.
Without You everything just seems
a mere illusion, just a dream,
for You are natural reality.

41, 42) As friend to friend I'd frequently
address You so sarcastically
as "Krishna of the famous Yadu clan."
So blind to Your true majesty,
how could I think so casually
and treat You as an ordinary man?
I joked with You and spoke with You
with disrespectful attitude.
I roamed with You, my mind in reverie.
Alone or not, I didn't mind
to rest with You as You reclined.
Forgive My insolent audacity.

43) The whole creation comes from You,
the moving and non-moving too,
our revered Guru, father, all-empowered.
Nobody else can interfere
or merge with You or be Your peer,
for You possess immeasurable power.

44) Repeatedly I fall before
Your lotus feet, my sovereign Lord,
the revered Deity of everyone.
I beg Your mercy. Otherwise
there's no escape from my demise.
Forgive me as a father would his son.

45) As friends forgive a friend's transgressions,
lovers pardon indiscretions,
please excuse my culpability.
O Lord of universal scope,
be gracious now. I simply hope
that somehow, You'll be satisfied with me.

46) Please show again Your four-armed form
as Vishnu that I've known before,
with lotus flower, conch shell, mace, and wheel.
From four-armed Vishnu has emerged
this form that fills the universe,
this thousand-armed expansion You've revealed.

47,48) *Lord Krishna said*:
Arjuna, as you now have asked,
My cosmic form has been unmasked,
this wondrous universal form of Mine.
And by My mystic potency
you've seen what no one else could see,
creation as it manifests in time.
Before you, none have seen the sight
of universal glaring light
that My primeval cosmic form divests.
No person can obtain this sight
by Vedic study, sacrifice,
austerity or charity or quest.
O best among the Kuru clan,

you've witnessed what no other can
wherever these three worlds are manifest.[XXVII]

49) You have become so troubled by
this ghastly cosmic form of Mine.
Just seeing it, you're mesmerized and burned.
So let this form now disappear
and once again you'll have no fear.
Be peaceful as My endless form returns.

50) *Sañjaya said:*
Lord Krishna, having spoken to
Arjuna in this calming mood
again displayed His four-armed Vishnu form.
Though it was wonderful and sweet,
so transcendentally complete,
Lord Krishna nonetheless again transformed.
Arjuna at this time was shown
Lord Krishna's form, His very own
exquisite and eternal two-armed form.
On seeing this familiar sight,
Arjuna felt his heart grow light.
Encouraged, he began to speak once more.[29]

51) *Arjuna said:*
As You are now appearing as a normal human man,
You're showing Me, Janārdana, a form I understand.

29 Krishna, not wishing Arjuna's mood to shift from friendship to fear, resumes His familiar form and continues teaching Arjuna about devotional service.

Now once again my mind assumes a natural repose
and I am feeling steady, calm, and so much more composed.

52) *Lord Krishna said*:
In fact, My own two-handed form is difficult to see.
Remember now as you refocus, standing next to Me,
that Lord Brahmā, Lord Shiva, and the gods can rarely find
what My devotees understand with pure and loving minds.

53) My own two-handed form is seen with transcendental eyes,
and not through faithful Vedic study favored by the wise.
The paths of Vedic mantras, penances, and charity
will all prove insufficient means for those in search of Me.

54) Unmixed devotion, nothing else, will make one qualified
to enter the Supreme abode, that place where I reside.
And only My devoted servants enter and perceive
My everlasting pastimes in their true reality.

55) The best among all *dharmas*[XXVIII] is to undertake to serve
and link with Me as My devoted, loving servitor.
Devotees have no enemies and purely understand
that they are dear to Me. For them, I'm always close at hand.

Bhaktivedanta Swami thus recites śrī-gītār gān
to please the pure devotees always rapt in Krishna's song.

Thus ends the eleventh chapter of Śrimad Bhagavad-gītā *named*
viśwarūpa-darśana-yoga *or The Universal Form.*

Chapter 12

Devotional Service

(bhakti-yoga)

1) *Arjuna said*:

O Krishna, I've another question. Kindly now respond.
Should one seek pure devotion, or should one pursue Brahman?
To worship the unmanifest transcends mundane desires.
Is proper service in devotion definitely higher?[30]

2) *Lord Krishna replied*:

A faithful servant fixed upon My personal appearance
is surely better off than the unmanifest adherents.
Their hearts, indeed, their very lives engaged in pleasing Me,
devotees are the topmost yogis. That is guaranteed.

3,4) Yet those who choose to worship the unmanifest Brahman—
the state that is immovable, unchanging, and beyond
all common understanding—can achieve self-mastery.
They're equally disposed to all and slowly come to Me.

5) The only difference in these paths is ease of execution.
Devotees progress easily while mystics face confusion.
Pursuing the unmanifest while dealing with a body
creates a slew of troubles for the seeker of *samādhi*.[XXIX]

6,7) Devotees render service as they meditate on Me.
They dedicate their life and heart in each activity.

---

30 Brahman refers to the impersonal, formless, all-pervading presence of God. To realize Brahman means to put a temporary stop to one's individuality and 'merge with God.' While Brahman realization is a legitimate path, Krishna describes it as *kleśa*, very difficult, because it requires unnatural withdrawal from others and is thus unsustainable. As Krishna explains in this chapter, *bhakti yoga* is easier because it can be added to one's current life and gradually developed in a sustainable, organic way.

Released from speculation and from craving the mundane,
they quickly are delivered from this world of death and pain.

8) So therefore, fix your mind on My two-handed form as the
essential form of Godhead in full Personality.
Stay linked with My eternal form and love of God will bloom,
advancement in one's life that is the greatest of all boons.

9) But if you cannot simply fix your consciousness on Me,
then offer service in devotion systematically.
Regardless if it's born of love or yogic regulation,
such service quickly brings one into My association.

10) And if you cannot render service so straightforwardly,
convert your normal work into an offering for Me.
To labor for Me in this way invokes My satisfaction
and draws you to Me due to ever-ripening attraction.

11) If you're too weak to work for Me and care not for devotion,
there yet remains another path to spiritual promotion.
Instead of simply working in a selfish way, begin
to do some work for others and be satisfied within.

12) To summarize, to serve in pure ecstatic love is best.
If that's too much, by practicing devotion you'll progress.
If that's too much, then study, as the learned souls suggest.
If that's too much, to meditate within yourself is next.
If that's too much, some action linked to God is still success,

for lusty, selfish actions never bring you happiness.
In summary, for peace of mind, renounce all selfishness.[31]

13,14) My pure devotees always manifest good qualities.
They're kind to everybody else and have no jealousy.
Non-envious and seeing soul ahead of the mundane,
devotees can compassionately fathom others' pain.
Devotees know that everything belongs to the Supreme.
Devotees do without the common egoistic dreams.
Devotees are self-satisfied and resolute to serve,
engaged in pleasing Me, their equanimity preserved.
By offering their mind, their life, their intellect to Me,
these dear, beloved servants stay perpetually free.

15) They never coerce others into some adversity.
They never bring to others mental pain or misery.
By always keeping balanced through both happiness and grief,
My dear, beloved servitors are always linked with Me.

16) Continually balanced, unaffected and carefree,
remaining independent of mundane society,
proficient, pure, and wise in day-to-day activities,
a soul becomes a *Vaiṣṇava*[XXX], forever dear to Me.

17) By neither celebrating nor lamenting mundane things,
by neither giving in to greed or needless worrying,
renouncing the auspicious and the inauspicious too,
devotees garner My respect and love in all they do.

31 Having presented options for progressively developing devotion, Krishna concludes this chapter by describing those who have achieved it.

18, 19) Again, please hear as I describe My faithful devotee,
who sees others as spirit, not as friend or enemy.
Impartial and adjusted both in fame and infamy,
untouched by heat and cold, by happiness or misery,
consistent in self-knowledge, shunning harmful company,
content with very simple things in quiet harmony,
detached from any dwelling, My determined devotee
forever renders service and is very dear to Me.

20) The spotless souls who practice pure devotion in this way
connecting with Me properly, their hearts imbued with faith,
will savor nectar free of gross material dismay.
To Me, these precious souls and I are very much the same.[32]

Bhaktivedanta Swami thus recites śrī-gītār gān
to please the pure devotees always rapt in Krishna's song.

Thus ends the twelfth chapter of Śrimad Bhagavad-gītā *named*
bhakti-yoga, *devotional service.*

32 While those who seek Brahman realization desire to become one with the Supreme, here, Krishna concludes that true oneness with the Supreme results from entering a loving relationship and becoming one in purpose with the Supreme Personality of Godhead, Sri Krishna.

Chapter 13

Nature, the Enjoyer and Consciousness

(prakṛti-puruṣa-viveka-yoga)

1) *Arjuna said*:
O killer of the Keshi fiend, about the spirit soul,
what is the field of action that he thinks he can control?
And what is nature? Who enjoys it? How does one expand
this theory to reality? Please help me understand.[33]

2) *Lord Krishna said*:
O son of Kuntī, I shall gladly answer your appeal.
The soul is called the knower of the body, or the field.

3) And at the same time, son of Bhārata, know I as well
can understand all bodies in which living spirits dwell.
For as the Supersoul I see each soul and all they do,
and that is perfect realization, from My point of view.

4) Now listen as I clarify and help you realize
how both the knower and the field are basically comprised,
as well as their appearance, what induces things they do,
and where the field and knower were initially produced.

5) Since learned sages write of this in ancient Vedic hymns,
from *Śri Vedānta-sūtra*, our discussion shall begin.

---

33 The first six chapters of *Bhagavad-gītā* deal with *karma yoga*, the yoga of action. The next six explain *bhakti yoga*, the yoga of devotion. Now we come to the final six, in which Krishna details *jñana yoga*, the yoga of knowledge. These chapters on *jñāna yoga* demonstrate that the devotional experience of *bhakti* is firmly rooted in knowledge beyond blind faith and sentiment.

Throughout the text, *Bhagavad-gītā* emphasizes *bhakti* as the highest yoga. The first six and last six chapters covering, respectively, *karma* and *jñāna yoga*, are compared to slices of sandwich bread buffering *bhakti*, the essential, identifying content.

Because these timeless writings aim to benefit mankind,
it's best that one accepts them and leaves other paths behind.

6,7) The field is matter: water, earth and six more subtle kinds,
the air and fire, ether, ego, reason, and the mind.
These manifest from their unmanifest totality.
We next count ten gross organs with distinct abilities:
the nose, the tongue, the skin, the eyes, and ears that gather facts;
the anus, stomach, arms and legs and genitals that act.
Five sense objects are counted next; aroma, form, and sound,
as well as taste and touch. These sensate items center round
the mind in action as a sense, thus making twenty-four.
From there, the spirit interacting with the flesh adds more,
including hatred, happiness, desire, stress, conviction
and bodies made of grossly elemental composition,
with life symptoms arising from the spirit soul inside.
Such is the field in which the knower of the field resides.

A learned soul who understands this full analysis
will know the gross and subtle parts of which the field consists.

8-12) And now I shall explain to you what knowledge means to Me.
A truly learned person manifests these qualities:
humility; a lack of pride; the practice of nonviolence;
submission to a guru teaching spiritual science;
tolerance; simplicity; a taste for being clean;
steadiness and self-control; a mind always serene;
knowledge and detachment from the evils of this life;

a less attached relationship with husband or with wife;
receiving joy and sorrow with an equal attitude;
acceptance of a life alone in quiet solitude;
respect and admiration for the endless quest for truth—
pursue these forms of knowledge. From all else remain aloof.

13) I now shall clarify the spirit, known as the Brahman.
The soul who knows this suitably drinks nectar on and on.
Brahman lies in My shelter and is called beginningless.
It stretches past all ordinary causes and effects.

14) Existing everywhere with form, including legs and hands,
with countless heads and eyes and ears and mouths to understand,
Brahman, here as the Supersoul, is always in our midst.
Without Him, not a thing within the three worlds would exist.

15) Providing others' senses, yet without senses Himself,
detached and yet at work maintaining everybody else,
creating all three modes and yet transcendent to their pull,
the ultimate enjoyer is the endless Supersoul.

16) Within and without every being, ambulant or still,
He's far away from everyone, yet very near as well.
He's much too subtle to perceive, to witness or to know,
and yet, in truth, He is reality, the Supersoul.

17) Without division and yet situated in each being,
He's fully self-contained and yet involved in everything.

One's birth, existence and demise are under His control.
And such is the eternal master known as Supersoul.

18) He instigates the brilliance of the sunshine, stars, and moon.
His light is fully spiritual, beyond the brightest noon.
Of things that can be known He is the object, source, and goal.
Forever in the hearts of all is He, the Supersoul.

19) The knowable, the knowledge and the field, I've now described.
I'm very fond of pandits for whom this is realized.
The soul who understands these truths devotes himself to Me,
absorbed in loving service in complete security.

20) While spirit souls, the living beings, know their tiny fields,
the Supersoul knows everybody. No one is concealed.
Dead matter and the living souls are both beginningless,
though nature and the modes transform them as they coexist.

21) The souls in this world make their varied efforts to enjoy
as nature forces causes and effects they can't avoid.

22) The soul therefore aligns with his material abode
while trying to enjoy under the spell of nature's modes.
He takes his birth repeatedly in high or lowly forms
while meeting good and evil as his outer shell transforms.

23) Embedded with the soul is Supersoul, who oversees
and permits all the soul pursues as birth and death proceed.

The owner, the controller, and the beneficiary,
the Supersoul uplifts the soul whose wisdom has been buried.

24) And only one who understands how living entities
attempt to mix with matter and its threefold energies,
resulting in another birth and sorrow it portends,
can overcome conditioning and not take birth again.

25) Devotees see the Supersoul in constant fascination,
attaining Him within themselves through loving meditation.
Empiric yogis analyze to understand the truth
while karma-yogis offer God their work and all its fruits.

26) Bereft of sacred wisdom, some move forward, nonetheless.
By hearing of and worshiping the Lord, they too progress.
A common person so inclined eventually transcends
by hearing from authorities, as scriptures recommend.

27) Yes, moving or non-moving, as one's outer form congeals,
it's just the field of action and the knower of that field.

28) A soul who sees the Supersoul in every entity,
established deep within the heart, is fortunate indeed.
For those who see reality know Supersoul prevails.
Forever indestructible, He cannot be curtailed.

29) Discovering the equal presence of the Supersoul,
one understands He's everywhere and always in control.

Such yogis never fall, for they are spiritually aligned
and overcome degrading urges from the rascal mind.

30) If one sees field and knower from the proper point of view
and sees that everything that bodies and their senses do
come only from the modes of natures' false supremacy
while souls in fact do nothing—such a person truly sees.

31) When one does not see others with diverse identities
defined by different bodies and their different properties,
one surely grows empowered to be mystically aware
and see that living spirits are expanded everywhere.

32) The knowers of the soul see endless, transcendental truth
above the realm of matter. Thus, they too remain aloof.

33) Just as the all-pervading sky
is subtle as it underlies
all things without becoming intermixed,
so does the soul pervade the flesh
while separate and not enmeshed,
a seed of consciousness, forever fixed.
Transcendent, blissful, in *samādhi*,
witnessing the active body
unentangled, realized souls exist.

34) As one unmoving sun distributes light through outer space,
or one unmoving king rules lands beyond his palace gates,

the single soul, O Son of Bhārata, illuminates
the mortal frame with consciousness while sitting in one place.

35) For those with eyes of knowledge every truth shall be revealed.
A learned soul can separate the knower and the field.
A learned soul perceives the soul and Supersoul within.
A learned soul sees how his liberation can begin.
Such learned souls transcend their mortal bodies when they die
and live in bliss forever in the spiritual sky.

Bhaktivedanta Swami thus recites śrī-gītār gān
to please the pure devotees always rapt in Krishna's song.

Thus ends the thirteenth chapter of Śrimad Bhagavad-gītā *named*
prakṛti-puruṣa-viveka-yoga, *nature, the enjoyer and consciousness.*

Chapter 14

The Three Modes of Material Nature

(guṇaṭraya-vibhāga-yoga)

1) *Lord Krishna said:*
Again I'll speak of knowledge bringing further benefits,
instructions far surpassing any others that exist.
The venerated sages of each era, each direction,
have ascertained this knowledge to attain complete perfection.

2) A person who obtains this knowledge sheds the mundane modes
and comes to transcendental life like Mine in My abode.
Such persons needn't tolerate a birth at the creation
nor death when all the cosmos undergoes annihilation.

3) Creation is the time when mortal beings take their birth
from pre-existing matter, such as water, flame, and earth.
Such matter, son of Bhārata, impregnated by Me,
then manifests a body for each living entity.

4) It's therefore understood that varied species of all kinds
have come about when I and mundane nature have combined.
While matter is the mother who creates one physically,
as Father, and the shelter of all souls, I give the seed.[34]

5) *Prakṛti*, nature, comes in modes of goodness, dark and passion
and forces the embodied soul to act in different fashions.
When these three modes infect the soul, he misidentifies
with his acquired body, and his bondage multiplies.

34 In previous chapters Krishna has mentioned the modes of material nature, and now He explains them in detail.

6) Among the modes, the mode of goodness stands out as most pure.
The mode of goodness, clear and bright, allows one to secure
both truth and knowledge, making one a bit too self-assured.
Entrapped by goodness, one believes his wisdom most mature.

7) The mode of passion causes greed and limitless desire
which leads to struggle, profit, loss, and grief till one expires.
Pursuits in passion steer the soul to things he can't attain
and strand him in an endless loop of happiness and pain.

8) And ignorance, the darkest mode, produces subtle bonds
that lead to madness, indolence, and sleeping on and on.

9) The soul entrapped in goodness gains a false sense of fulfillment.
In passion he gains selfishness, in darkness, mental illness.

10) At times the mode of goodness pushes out both dark and passion,
and sometimes passion forces dark and goodness to inaction.
Then darkness pushes good and passion to obscurity.
In this way each unbalanced mode pursues supremacy.

11) When goodness dominates, its influence at once dispenses
both knowledge and enlightenment to all the body's senses.

12) When passion dominates, a person's normal disposition
evolves into a craving for respect and grand positions.

13) And when the mode of darkness dominates, its strong assertion
will leave a person lost, confused, and crippled with inertia.
O son of Kuru, all these traits are easily perceived
as all three modes of nature drive the soul's activities.[35]

14) The modes determine what will happen when the body dies.
A death in goodness leads to worlds where sinless souls reside.

15) To die in passion leads to birth with lusty, greedy men.
To die in darkness makes a man an animal again.

16) Those actions in the mode of goodness make one purified,
while actions born of passion makes one's sorrow magnified.
And foolish actions born of ignorance are surely worst,
for they move humans to the realm of beasts in the next birth.

17) While goodness brings real knowledge, passion brings voracity,
and darkness brings illusion, chaos, and insanity.

18) Those souls in goodness go to heaven, those in dark to hell,
and those in passion stay on Earth, which suits them very well.

---

35 After this overview of the modes, now and through the rest of this *jñāna yoga* portion of *Bhagavad-gītā*, Krishna explains their influence over these facets of life:
Chapter 14: Death, actions, and destinations after death.
Chapter 17: Faith, foods, sacrifice, austerity, and charity.
Chapter 18: Renunciation, knowledge, actions (again), the actor, understanding, determination, and happiness.

19) When one can see the modes alone steer every kind of work,
when one can see the subtle powers they alone assert,
and when one sees Me and My service where the modes can't reach,
one then starts to organically attain My qualities.

20) The modes comprise the body, and so when the soul transcends,
the bondages of illness, aging, birth and death will end.

21) *Arjuna said*:
Beloved Lord, if one transcends the modes, how is it shown?
Just what is one's behavior when the modes are overthrown?

22-25) *Lord Krishna said*:
Such persons see enlightenment and ignorance alike,
the modes producing causes and effects of different types.
Although in these three worlds, discord and hankering are rife,
a transcendental person stays detached throughout his life.
And even when the modes are active, one who is mature
is always transcendental, unconcerned, and undisturbed.
With such detachment, sober souls, unmoved by joy or pain,
perceive a lump of earth or gold as more or less the same.
Unchanged by both adverse and helpful things that come their way,
they see both friend and foe alike, as well as shame and praise.
Enjoyment and renunciation, neither to extreme,
depict a person transcendental to the modes' regime.

26) If one just acts in full devotion, always serving Me
one overcomes the modes of nature most assuredly.

Devotees who stay steadily and constantly engaged

will rise above dull matter to the *brahma-bhūta*[XXXI] stage.

27) For I'm the very basis upon which Brahman exists,

that vast, amorphous state that is forever full of bliss.

I am the shelter of Brahman, which many seek to gain,

though service to Me in devotion rarely is attained.

Bhaktivedanta Swami thus recites śrī-gītār gān
to please the pure devotees always rapt in Krishna's song.

Thus ends the fourteenth chapter of Śrimad Bhagavad-gītā *named* guṇaṭraya-vibhāga-yoga*, the three modes of material nature.*

Chapter 15

The Yoga of the Supreme Person

(puruṣottama-yoga)

1) *Lord Krishna said*:

Those men who read the Vedas with the goal of fruitive gain
shall reappear in lower species, ever to remain.
Their life is like an endless banyan, never falling down,
its roots protruding skyward and its branches to the ground.
The flowery Vedic hymns comprise this tree's confusing leaves
that fabricate illusions universally believed.

2) With dictates from the modes of nature giving them nutrition,
the branches from this tree extend in up and down positions.
Each branch provides conditioned souls sense objects to enjoy
along with many miseries they never can avoid.
Conditioned souls meander through the branches of this tree
pursuing worldly pleasure in mundane society.

3, 4) As men of lesser intellect can neither see the end
of endless skies above them nor from where the skies begin,
conditioned souls cannot conceive the true form of this tree,
condemning them to struggle in its grip perpetually.
The roots of this great tree cannot be cut by any force
and thousands of mistakes arise when fools attempt that course.
The single weapon of detachment only can succeed
in cutting down this strongly rooted worldly banyan tree.
On having cut this tree, the soul is fortunate and blessed
to search out and attain reality and truthfulness.
Such souls attain Vaikuṇṭha planets, never to return,
for God Himself is by this banyan's root, they come to learn.

And thus the wise surrender to the Lord who manifests
all things at any time that anything at all exists.[36]

5) Released from false prestige, deceit, and bad association,
detached from lust, discerning fixed and changing situations,
the soul untouched by joy or sorrow leaves the worldly modes
and reaches, in surrender, the eternal Lord's abode.

6) No sunshine is required to illuminate that place,
and nor is fire, voltage, or the moon in outer space.
My infinite abode is such that if one enters in,
one never wants to see a mundane residence again.

7) The numberless eternal souls are spirit sparks of Mine,
existing in this world where they are physically entwined.
Their restless minds and senses keep them tightly wrapped and bound
and struggling to find some joy where little can be found.

8) Accepting situations born from mother after mother,
the fallen souls seek pleasure in one body or another.
As wind moves many fragrances, the spirit soul collects
conceptions of enjoyment in this body and the next.

9) Enjoying mind and senses with desires at the helm,
the soul proceeds to see and taste and touch and hear and smell.

36 In this chapter Krishna describes the entangling material energy and how to get out of it. He then differentiates between souls who escape material entanglement, those who don't, and He Himself.

Conditioned souls thus hanker for, according to their birth,
a set of sensate objects as they roam about the Earth.

10) Repeated births and deaths are all these foolish souls attain.
Enchanted by their bodies, they see nothing more to gain.
But if one has a kindly guru, all of this can change,
for birth and death are evident to one whose eyes are trained.

11) So many yogis use techniques that lack this point of view.
Rebirth and death encircle them, no matter what they do.
But those who are self-realized, whose consciousness is pure,
begin to see the soul as their enlightenment matures.

12) The endless, brilliant sunshine that pervades the whole creation,
and all the splendid moonbeams that obscure the constellations,
can only give their light because of My authority.
The light of anyone enlightened also comes from Me.

13) This planet and its atmosphere remain afloat in space
due only to My energy and all-pervading grace.
Varieties of vegetables and herbs can all survive
because of shining moonlight that I steadily supply.

14) As well, I am the life air as it enters and retreats,
enabling all beings to digest the food they eat.

15) Established deep in every heart,
as Supersoul I then impart

a person's knowledge and their memory.
I help a person recollect
or force a person to forget.
Forgetfulness itself has come from Me.
In this world, all the Vedic texts
direct the seeker to reflect
and gradually come to knowing Me.
Eventually, I alone
by all the Vedas can be known,
for I compiled and know them. Listen, please.

16) Each living entity exists in one of two positions;
the free souls live in My abode, while others are conditioned.
The liberated souls possess infallibility,
while others remain fallible until they live with Me.

17) Besides these two there is the Greatest Personality,
the Supersoul, controlling and pervading all that be.

18) Because I am that transcendental Personality,
infallible and fallible do not apply to Me.

19) The one who understands Me as the Personal Supreme
is free of doubts and knows Me as the best of everything.
That person, having understood the Vedic paradigm,
will serve Me well, in heartfelt pure devotion, all the time.

20) Please hear these deep and secret *śastric*[XXXII] topics and begin

to purify your mind and cleanse your actions of all sin.

O son of Bhārat, one who knows these secrets, blessed and wise,

achieves perfection in pursuit of any enterprise.

Bhaktivedanta Swami thus recites śrī-gītār gān
to please the pure devotees always rapt in Krishna's song.

Thus ends the fifteenth chapter of Śrimad Bhagavad-gītā *named* purușottama-yoga, *the yoga of the supreme person.*

Chapter 16

The Divine and Demonic Natures

(daivāsura-sampada-vibhāga-yoga)

1-3) *Lord Krishna said:*
My dear Arjuna, godly souls possess these qualities:
pursuit of education, fearlessness, simplicity,
sacrifice, self-discipline, a life of purity,
study of the Vedas, generous gifts of charity,
honesty, nonviolence, no anger without cause,
peacefulness, detachment, a dislike for finding flaws,
gentleness, compassion for another person's needs,
energy, humility, indifference to greed,
cleanliness, endurance, grace, steadfast determination,
forgiveness, and an absence of the lust for adoration.
These twenty-six transcendent qualities surely define
a person born of godly nature, blessed by the divine.

4) The demons, on the other hand, are arrogant and vain.
Though merciless, irate, and ignorant, they have no shame.

5) While transcendental qualities promote one's liberation,
demonic qualities impose nonstop reincarnation.
O son of Pāṇḍu, none of this should agitate your mind,
for you are surely born with qualities of the divine.

6) O Son of Bhārat, two distinctive beings fill this world.
The first is the divine, of which you've now already heard.
The others are demonic, and quite often they prevail.
Now hear as I describe the demon's ways in more detail.[37]

---

37 Having compared materialistic life to an endless banyan tree, Krishna now describes the harsh mentality of bewildered souls determined to exploit the fruits of this tree.

7) The demons don't know what is right or what is wrong to do.
They're filthy, misbehaved, and unconcerned with what is true.

8) The demons say there is no God, rejecting on the whole
a personal creator with unlimited control.
Instead they look upon this world as nothing more than just
an accident or happenstance arising out of lust.

9) With such a stunted vision, demons fail to ascertain
their own identity because they lack sufficient brains.
And so they turn to ghastly work devoid of benefits
that causes much destruction through demonic influence.

10) Resorting to unending lust, bewildered by conceit,
illusioned demons vow to finish filthy, fleeting deeds.

11,12) Persistent fear and apprehension dominate the lives
of those whose hearts seek only to keep passions satisfied.
Entangled in a thousand wants they struggle to fulfill,
the demons, pushed by lust and anger, strive to stuff their tills.
Accumulating money by illegal, horrid means,
the demons utilize their minds for reprehensive schemes.

13-16) The demon thinks, "Today I'm rich, fulfilling my desires.
Tomorrow will be perfect. Even more shall I acquire.
That enemy is dying and another I shall kill,
for I am rich and bend all things according to my will.
Yes, I am the enjoyer, always perfect, strong, and pleased.

No other in the world can be content and glad like me.
Although my wealthy relatives surround me on all sides,
among them, who could ever be as glorious as I?
Now let me do some ritual, some public charity,
and then I'll find some women for my private ecstasy."

Reflecting thus, the demon feeds illusions in his mind,
ignoring how his lifetime dwindles in the grip of time.
Distorted and entangled by desires he can't quell,
the demon heads directly to his residence in hell.

17) Conceited and enamored with prestige and excess wealth,
the demon stays complacent and absorbed upon himself.
The sacrifices he performs, bereft of regulations,
are only hollow rituals to build his reputation.

18) Absorbed in their false ego, power, anger, lust, and pride,
the demons become jealous of My presence deep inside.
Perceiving only bodies, they resent the qualities
displayed by saintly persons, whom they blaspheme endlessly.[38]

19) Malicious, jealous demons, who are lowest among men
are cast to dismal births and deaths again and yet again.

20) Attaining birth in wicked species, demons spend their lives
in useless, hapless actions the demonic life derives.
By overlooking Me, these fools are endlessly confined

38 Krishna now contrasts the destinations of the demon and the devotee.

to births and deaths of misery and torment all the time.
As step by step each lifetime becomes more detestable,
the chance of making Me their goal becomes impossible.

21) Resentment, lust, and greed comprise three gateways to this hell.
The saints renounce these three and thus live peacefully and well.

22) Now hear, O son of Kuntī, of such persons who are free
from these three gates to darkness and ensuant infamy.
They always seek religious work of highest pedigree
and gain self-realization through their service unto Me.

23) If someone gives up sacred guidance, acting lustfully,
they never gain perfection, joy, or lasting liberty.

24) And therefore, through the scriptures, one should clearly understand
both beneficial actions and those actions that are banned.

Bhaktivedanta Swami thus recites śrī-gītār gān
to please the pure devotees always rapt in Krishna's song.

Thus ends the sixteenth chapter of Śrimad Bhagavad-gītā *named*
daivāsura-sampada-vibhāga-yoga, *the divine and demonic natures.*

Chapter 17

The Divisions of Faith

(śraddhāṭraya-vibhāga-yoga)

1) *Arjuna said*:
O Krishna, what becomes of those who worship as they please
without parameters from scriptural authorities?
Is random worship ignorant or passionate or good?
Please tell me the details about this matter if you would. [39]

2) *Lord Krishna said*:
According to the modes that the embodied soul acquires,
his faith appears in one of the three modes, as he desires.
Now listen to Me carefully and you shall understand
that any faith one has arises from the modes' commands.

3) O son of Bhārata, as the three modes exert their sway,
one manifests and comes to hold a certain type of faith.

4) And as the modes advance one's faith in various directions,
one soon begins to worship as a natural progression.
A soul in goodness worships gods and all the godly host
while one in passion worships demons, one in darkness, ghosts.

5,6) Some men perform austerities devoid of Vedic guides
that really come from lust, attachment, arrogance, and pride.
Compelled to fast excessively by vanity alone,
such fools impose much misery upon their flesh and bones.
Tormenting both the body and the Supersoul within,
such penance is demonic from the outset to the end.

---

39 Many people consider themselves 'spiritual but not religious.' This chapter deals with the value of taking spiritual direction from the *Vedas* as opposed to creating one's own ideas of spirituality, ideas inevitably influenced by the modes of material nature.

7) The modes of nature impact men in everything they do,
as when they are selecting, for example, favorite foods.
The modes will also manifest in three varieties
in terms of sacrifice, austerity, and charity.

8-10) In goodness, food increases life span, vigor, joy, and taste.
Such juicy, fatty, pleasing foods look nice upon their plates.
In passion, food creates disease. With too much salt or heat,
it's bitter, sour, arid, burnt, and difficult to eat.
In darkness, food is rotten, tasteless, leftover, and old.
Emitting putrid odors, it is often eaten cold.

11) A sacrifice that's dutiful, with scriptural decree,
is in the mode of goodness and presented selflessly.

12) A sacrifice done pridefully with benefits in mind
is in the mode of passion, a subsidiary kind.

13) But sacrifice in ignorance, devoid of hymns and feasts,
is faithless and capricious and has unrewarded priests.

14-17) Austerities in goodness, the unselfish, sacred kind,
include those of the body, of the voice, and of the mind.
The worship of the Lord, the priests, the guru, and the saints
with cleanliness, simplicity, and sexual restraint,
are all ideal austerities of bodily domains.
That speech that does not agitate, that pleases and explains,
while citing Vedic scriptures by deliberative choice

comprises the austerity pertaining to the voice.
And satisfaction, self-control, solemnity, and ease
describe the mind in goodness and its own austerities.

18) Austerities performed for profit, pride, prestige, and praise
are passionate, the scriptures say, with fruits that fade away.

19) Austerities in foolishness that mortify the flesh,
exposing everyone involved to danger and distress,
are ignorant, the scriptures say. Though done extensively,
such penances don't help because they're just illusory.

20-22) In goodness, charity is always given selflessly
at proper times and places, and to one exemplary.
In passion, charity is given only for return,
presented very grudgingly, without sincere concern.
And charity in ignorance is given without grace
to one who is unworthy, at improper time and place.

23) The venerated brahmans, following scriptural decree,
observed their vows of penance, sacrifice, and charity
along with other practices of proven piety
while chanting, "*Oṁ tat sat*," connecting all to the Supreme.

24) Thus any transcendental practice brahmans may pursue
begins with '*Oṁ*' to verify it's absolutely true.

25) While those desiring *mokṣā*[XXXIII] may progress materially
from practicing their penance, sacrifice, and charity,
those persons seeking bhakti also undertake these three
but only for the cause of satisfying the Supreme.

26, 27) '*Sat*' means the eternal, absolute, transcendent truth.
To work for the Supreme is similarly absolute.
One's penance, sacrifice and charity are meant for Him
when either done in worldly ways or through the Vedic hymns.

28) An action undertaken without faith in the Supreme
the Vedic scriptures call "*asat*," a vain, fallacious dream.
Such actions, inconsistent with the sacred Vedic texts,
bear fruits that bring no benefit in this life or the next.

Bhaktivedānta Swāmi thus recites śrī-gītār gān
to please the pure devotees always rapt in Krishna's song.

Thus ends the seventeenth chapter of Śrimad Bhagavad-gītā *named*
śraddhāṭraya-vibhāga-yoga, *the divisions of faith.*

Chapter 18

Conclusion: The Perfection of Renunciation

(mokṣa-yoga)

1) *Arjuna said*:
O Krishna, master of the senses, please explain to me
how true renunciates maintain their equanimity.
Please make the very purpose of renunciation clear.
Whenever You explain something, I always love to hear.[40]

2) *Lord Krishna said*:
Renunciation means to stop pursuing consequences
meant only to appease one's aggravating mundane senses.
Experience allows a person to delineate
both true renunciation and the true renunciate.

3) Some learned people say to give up all activity,
while others counsel penance, sacrifice, and charity.

4) O best among the Bhāratas, consider My decision:
tyāga, or renunciation, has its three divisions.

5) One never should abandon sacrifice and charity
for everybody benefits from such activities.
The greatest souls will never set such worthy acts aside,
for through such pious actions even they are purified.

6) But sacrifice and charity should not be done for gain.
When done from duty, their full value can be ascertained.

---

40 A renunciate (*sannyasi*) would ordinarily not fight in a battle. Since Krishna has rebuffed Arjuna's initial idea of renouncing by leaving the battle, Arjuna wants to know how he could fight and yet be renounced.

7) One's stipulated duties should be taken up at once.
Renouncing them outright is just the mode of ignorance.

8) Renouncing duties out of fear of trouble or distress
is evidence the influence of passion has progressed.
As many lessons from the sacred writings have foretold,
renouncing in this way will never elevate the soul.

9) In goodness one performs his work as duty has prescribed,
renouncing all attachment to results the work provides.

10) A sensible renunciate proceeds in all conditions,
for even inauspicious work does not change his position.
The true renunciate remains in goodness constantly,
released from doubts and focused on prescribed activities.

11) Embodied souls cannot renounce their duties in this world,
but those who can renounce the fruits of work are undisturbed.

12) A man attached gets stuck in heaven, hell, or in between.
A man detached is free of karmic fruits that intervene.

13) O mighty-armed Arjuna, hear as I explain to you
five causes of your actions that influence all you do.
Vedānta sutra says these five shall always regulate
each action, good or bad, that anyone may undertake.

14) The soul who acts, the act itself, the body, all the senses,
and Supersoul—these five determine different consequences.

15) Whatever duties, speeches, thoughts, or actions one pursues,
regardless if they're right or wrong from other points of view,
these five factors decree if they are perfect or have flaws.
In every case, for everyone, there is no other cause.

16) The fools imagine they alone cause everything they do.
They never understand how these five influences rule.

17) So therefore, one released from ordinary vanity,
detached, intelligent, engaged in working selflessly,
may kill someone as duty with a higher motivation
without getting entangled in a karmic situation.

18) The knowledge and its object motivate the one who knows.
The senses, work, and doer govern how the action goes.

19) The knowledge, act, and actor are by three modes classified.
Now listen to their differences, as I shall summarize.

20) According to his nature, each embodied living being
desires fruits and thus transmutes to beast or human being.
When knowledge is in goodness one sees each eternal soul
as linked with every other, though distinct within the whole.

21) When knowledge is in passion every soul appears diverse
according to their body, some as better, some as worse.

22) When knowledge is in darkness, incorrect and very small,
one only sees the superficial body, that is all.

23) When action is in goodness it's detached and regulated
and always undertaken without sense of love or hatred.

24) When action is in passion, proudly done to please the senses,
it ends up being stressful, in both deed and consequences.

25) When action is in ignorance, the actor's unconcerned
that vicious and distressing acts bring bondage in return.

26) An actor fixed in goodness, both detached and self-possessed,
stays eager and determined throughout failure and success.

27) An actor caught in passion only thinks of what he'll gain.
He's envious, polluted and controlled by joy and pain.

28) An actor stuck in darkness, always lazy and delayed,
is selfish, stubborn, gloomy, rude and scorns what scriptures say.

29) O Dhanañjaya, hear of how the three modes take command
of one's determination and the way one understands.

30) That understanding in the mode of goodness helps one see
what should be done, what should be feared, and what will set one free.

31) To understand in passion means to fail to ascertain
when one should act by scripture and when one should just abstain.

32) To understand in darkness means one can't tell right from wrong,
for when the just appears unjust, one's acumen is gone.

33) Determination in the mode of goodness carries on
one's actions, life, and senses. It's unbreakable and strong.

34) Determination in the mode of passion always holds
to money, piety, and lust as worthwhile, selfish goals.

35) Determination in the mode of darkness simply stays
in foolish, fearful, phantom states of dreamy mental haze.

36) O best among the Bhāratas, please hear about the three
varieties of happiness that counter miseries.
One's happiness in this world is in fact illusory,
for every joy and sorrow is destroyed eventually.

37) That happiness in goodness may seem poisonous at first
yet ends up as refreshing nectar, satisfying thirst.
Such happiness enlightens one who has it more and more,
including one mistakenly in bodily rapport.

38) That happiness in passion puts the senses in a spin.
At first it tastes like nectar but it's poison at the end.

39) And happiness in darkness is delusion through and through.
Equating sleep and laziness with joy is just untrue.

40) The modes of nature's domineering influence extends
throughout the total universe, among both gods and men,

41) Subduer of the enemy, the modes alone create
one's priestly, business, labor, or administrative traits.

42) The peaceful *brāhmaṇs* naturally act with self-control.
Forbearance, knowledge, truth, and wisdom mark these godly souls.

43) The *kṣatriyas* or leader class, resourceful, brave, and stout,
are heroes who can shelter all and keep opponents out.

44) The *vaiśyas*, merchants, work with land and cows and then invest.
The *śūdras*, workers, labor in the service of the rest.

45) A person gains perfection just by following his nature
and driving out the modes through his inherent type of labor.

46) Perfecting one's own nature as one works for the Supreme,
one abdicates this world and its illusory regime.
The Lord is both the origin and ultimate provider
of everything, including both our life and our desire.

47) To do one's duty, even if the outcome's second class,
relieves the fear that comes from doing someone else's tasks.
To act by one's own nature in a sound, exclusive way,
removes sinful reactions, as the laws of scripture say.

48) Endeavors always have some fault, in total or in part,
yet one makes them more faultless keeping reverence in the heart.
In this world every deed has faults, no matter how inspired,
for fault surrounds each action just as smoke surrounds a fire.

49) By taking up one's duties as the modes make one inclined
and giving up demands the senses always seem to find,
a person grows detached and wise, empowered to surmount
the cravings that prevent one from becoming more renounced.[41]

50) Now hear about this perfect stage, as I shall summarize
just how Brahman, the Absolute, is fully realized.

51-53) Purified by wisdom, resolute and well engaged,
free from want and hatred, with the senses all restrained,
living simply, eating little, words and mind controlled,
practiced in detachment, ever focused on the soul,
free from anger, greed, false ego, bullying, and pride,
unattached to worldly life and all that it provides,

---

41 Having answered Arjuna's question about renunciation in great depth, Krishna has concluded the *jñāna yoga* portion of the *Bhagavad-gītā.* He now finishes His lessons to Arjuna with a strong, loving appeal to take to *bhakti yoga* followed by a surprising declaration of His own detachment.

peaceful with simplicity, proclaiming no regime—
in such a state one certainly can realize the Supreme.

54) In Brahman realization, transcendentalists have no
more hankering or sorrow. Jubilation overflows.
Displaying equal feelings toward each living entity,
one goes beyond the modes, attaining service unto Me.

55) Surpassing all three modes and serving Me exclusively,
one fathoms both My formlessness and personality.
Brahman, the Supersoul, and *Bhagavān*[XXXIV]—these three comprise
My multi-features known by those completely realized.

56) Established thus, one comes upon one's true identity
through transcendental loving service full of ecstasy.
By serving Me in many ways, My servant gains My grace
and soon attains to My abode, where endless bliss awaits.

57) While sheltered in this loving mood, be conscious about Me
and always execute devotional activities.
Engaged this way on My behalf and under My protection,
whatever you may do will lead to absolute perfection.

58) Remember Me and by My grace you'll easily surpass
the suffering and sorrow people in this world amass.
Conversely, if you disregard the words that I have said,
your ego will mislead you to destroy yourself instead.

59) And if your ego pushes you to dithering or flight,
you'll act upon a falsehood, for your nature is to fight.

60) All people are conditioned to their own activities.
O son of Kunti, heed your natural proclivities.
Give up these misconceptions that are causing your travail.
In time, your own inherent disposition will prevail.

61) Residing in the hearts of all, directing all they do,
the Lord Himself determines consequences that ensue.
He lets the spirit wander in a physical machine,
pursuing empty pleasures and imaginary dreams.

62) Surrender and find shelter at His gracious lotus feet.
Submit yourself to Him and your fulfillment is complete.
His mercy brings you lasting peace and fortune, rest assured,
for in His residence there is no anguish to endure.

63) My words are confidential and more confidential still.
Decide if you'll observe them or reject them, as you will.
Reflect again on all the good advice you have acquired.
Consider what I've said and do whatever you desire.[42]

64) Because you are My cherished friend, I'll share these final words,
a lesson still more intimate than all as yet you've heard.

42 Krishna finishes His instructions with a very personal request and invites Arjuna to share what he learned with qualified students.

65) Remember Me, give homage and devote yourself to Me.
In this way you will come to Me. You have My guarantee.

66) Abandon all religious creeds, surrender unto Me,
and I shall give you shelter and protect you constantly.
You never need be anxious over any past mistakes,
for in My shelter, transcendental peace predominates.

67) Indulgent, mundane, faithless souls who always seem to feel
that My transcendent, blissful form is factually unreal,
should never be instructed in these sacred words of Mine.
They cannot understand them and are not at all inclined.

68) But if you teach those persons with devotion unto Me,
your service and attainment of Myself are guaranteed.

69) Moreover, since no service is more dear to Me than this,
devotees teaching others relish transcendental bliss.

70) All those who somehow understand and study My advice
shall worship Me in knowledge, which itself is sacrifice.

71) And faithful souls who simply sit and hear these lessons well
attain auspicious planets wherein pious people dwell.

72) Have you now heard these principles attentively yourself?
Have all your doubts been answered now, O conqueror of wealth?

The dark and wretched burden of that ignorance you felt—
O son of Pṛthā, has all that been thoroughly dispelled?

73) *Arjuna said:*
O Krishna, my illusion is destroyed. You never fail.
My doubts have all been cleared away. My grief will not prevail.
Your mercy has delivered me. My memory is back.
Your words have made it clear that, as a warrior, I must act.[43]

74) *Sanjaya said:*
On hearing this discussion between Krishna and His friend,
the hairs across my body are all standing up on end.

75) The mercy of my guru Vyāsadeva let me hear
these confidential words by which Arjuna's mind was cleared.
Proceeding from the Lord of mysticism's lotus mouth,
these lessons are incomparable. Of this there is no doubt.

76) O King, as I recall these words again and yet again,
I marvel at their message and my ecstasy ascends.
Arjuna's talks with Keśava, a boon for all mankind,
shall always and repeatedly inspire those inclined.

43 Arjuna is now prepared to take up the battle with the same enthusiasm he initially felt when he ordered Krishna to drive his chariot between the armies. However, now his motive has completely changed. Previously he thought he was fighting for the throne. Now he knows he is fighting for Krishna.

Sanjaya concludes by expressing his own joy on hearing the *Bhagavad-gītā* and indirectly answers King Dhritarashtra's question from the opening verse.

77) Lord Krishna's wondrous form again appears within my mind,
delighting me and striking me with wonder every time.

78) Wherever there is Krishna, the supremely mystic Soul,
and anywhere Arjuna wields his arrows and his bow,
great power, wealth and triumph come, and learned souls proclaim
there is no real distinction between Krishna and His name.

Bhaktivedanta Swami thus recites śrī-gītār gān
to please the pure devotees always rapt in Krishna's song.

Thus ends the eighteenth chapter of Śrimad Bhagavad-gītā *named* moksa-yoga, *the perfection of renunciation.*

Oṁ tat sat.

Conclusion

Throughout his poetic *Gītār Gān*, Śrila Prabhupāda weaves in commentary to make the ancient text relevant for today's reader. In the final verse, he mentions the name of Krishna as non-different from Krishna, alluding to an earlier reference (10.25). Especially in this age of quarrel and confusion (*kali-yuga*), to easily apply the teachings of *Bhagavad-gītā*, one can chant the names of Krishna in the *māha-mantra*:

Hare Krishna Hare Krishna, Krishna Krishna, Hare Hare,
Hare Rama, Hare Rama, Rama Rama, Hare Hare.

This chanting was practiced and prescribed by Sri Caitanya Mahaprabhu, revered in sacred Vedic texts as Krishna's incarnation for *kali-yuga*. Sri Caitanya taught that although chanting any name of the Supreme purifies the chanter, the name of Krishna is the most direct.

Author's Note

This abridged version of *Gītār Gān* includes only the English translations of the text. The complete version of *Gītār Gān* contains:

- Word for word English translations of each Bengali stanza composed by Śrila Prabhupāda. (As a sample, Chapter 15 follows).

- Śrila Prabhupāda's poetic invocation, also translated to English word for word.

- An English translation of Śrila Prabhupāda's introduction explaining the importance of *Bhagavad-gītā* in various spiritual lineages.

The complete version will soon be available at sweetsongbooks.com.

Chapter 15

The Yoga of the Supreme Person

(puruṣottama-yoga)

1) *śrī-bhagavān kahilen:*
veda-vāṇī karma-kāṇḍī saṁsāra āśraye I
nānā yoni prāpta haya kabhu mukta naya II 1
saṁsāra ye vṛkṣa sei aśvattha avyaya I
ūrdhva-mūla adhaḥ-śākhā nāhi tāra kṣaya II 2
puṣpita vedera chanda se brahmera patra I
mohita se veda-vākya jagata sarvatra II 3

śrī-bhagavān – the Supreme Personality of Godhead; *kahilen* – said; *veda-vāṇī* – contents of the Vedas; *karma-kāṇḍī* – one who follows section regarding fruitive activities; *saṁsāra* – life; *āśraye* – in taking shelter; *nānā* – various; *yoni* – species; *prāpta* – attained; *haya* – there is; *kabhu* – ever; *mukta* – liberated; *naya* – not; *saṁsāra* – life; *ye* – that; *vṛkṣa* – tree; *sei* – that only; *aśvattha* – banyan tree; *avyaya* – eternal; *ūrdhva-mūla* – roots above; *adhaḥ* – downwards; *śākhā* – branches; *nāhi* – not; *tāra* – of that; *kṣaya* – destruction; *puṣpita* – flowery; *vedera* – of the Vedas; *chanda* – hymns; *se* – such; *brahmera* – of Brahmajyoti, the energy of the Lord; *patra* – leaves; *mohita* – under illusion; *se* – that; *veda* – of the Vedas; *vākya* – topics; *jagata* – universe; *sarvatra* – everywhere.

Lord Krishna said:
Those men who read the Vedas with the goal of fruitive gain
shall reappear in lower species, ever to remain.
Their life is like an endless banyan, never falling down,
its roots protruding skyward and its branches to the ground.
The flowery Vedic hymns comprise this tree's confusing leaves
that fabricate illusions universally believed.

2) *vṛkṣera se śākhāli ūrdhva adhaḥ-gati* I
guṇera vaśete yāra yathā vidhi-mati II 4
se vṛkṣera śākhā yata viṣayera bhoga I
nija karma anusāre yata bhava-roga II 5
baddha-jīva ghure sei vṛkṣa ḍāle ḍāle I
manuṣya-loka se bhuñje nija karma-phale II 6

vṛkṣera – of the tree; *se* – that; *śākhāli* – branches; *ūrdhva* – upwards; *adhaḥ* - downward; *gati* – growth; *guṇera* – of the three modes of material nature; *vaśete* – under influence; *yāra* – those who; *yathā* – when; *vidhi-mati* – as per rules; *se* – that; *vṛkṣera* – of the tree; *śākhā* – branches; *yata* – as many; *viṣayera* – of the objects of senses; *bhoga* – enjoyment; *nija* – own; *karma* – activities; *anusāre* – according to; *yata* – as many; *bhava-roga* – material miseries; *baddha-jīva* – conditioned soul; *ghure* – wander; *sei* – that only; *vṛkṣa* – tree; *ḍāle* – in branch; *ḍāle* – after branch; *manuṣya-loka* – the world of human society; *se* – that; *bhuñje* – enjoy; *nija* – own; *karma-phale* – in fruits of actions.

With dictates from the modes of nature giving them nutrition,
the branches from this tree extend in up and down positions.
Each branch provides conditioned souls sense objects to enjoy
along with many miseries they never can avoid.
Conditioned souls meander through the branches of this tree
pursuing worldly pleasure in mundane society.

3, 4) *kṣudra-buddhi manuṣya se sīmā nāhi pāya* I
ananta ākāśe tāra ādi anta naya II 7
kivā rūpa se vṛkṣera tāhā nāhi bujhe I
ananta-kālera madhye jīva yuddha yujhe II 8
se aśvattha vṛkṣa haya sudṛḍha ye mūla I
se mūla kāṭite haya śata śata bhula II 9
anāsakti eka astra se mūla kāṭite I
sei se ye dṛḍha astra saṁsāra jinite II 10
kāṭiyā se vṛkṣa-mūla satyera sandhāna I
bhāgya-krame yāra haya tāte avasthāna II 11
se yāya vaikuṇṭha-loke phire nāhi āse I

e vṛkṣera mūla yathā se puruṣa pāśe II 12
se ādi puruṣe adya kara se prapatti I
janmādi se yāhā hate prakṛti pravṛtti II 13

kṣudra – small quantity; *buddhi* – intelligent; *manuṣya* – human being; *se* – that; *sīmā* – limit; *nāhi* – not; *pāya* – receive; *ananta* – no end; *ākāśe* – in sky; *tāra* – of that; *ādi* – beginning; *anta* – end; *naya* – not; *kivā* – whatever; *rūpa* – form; *se* – that; *vṛkṣera* – of the tree; *tāhā* – such persons; *nāhi* – not; *bujhe* – understand; *ananta* – no end; *kālera* – of time; *madhye* – amidst; *jīva* – living being; *yuddha* – fight; *yujhe* – get engaged in; *se* – that; *aśvattha* – banyan; *vṛkṣa* – tree; *haya* – is; *sudṛḍha* – strong; *ye* – that; *mūla* – root; *se* – that; *mūla* – root; *kāṭite* – to cut; *haya* – there is; *śata* – thousands; *śata* – and thousands; *bhula* – of errors; *anāsakti* – detachment; *eka* – one; *astra* – weapon; *se* – that; *mūla* – root; *kāṭite* – to cut; *sei* – that only; *se* – such; *ye* – that; *dṛḍha* – strong; *astra* – weapon; *saṁsāra* – the world; *jinite* – to live; *kāṭiyā* – after cutting; *se* – that; *vṛkṣa* – tree; *mūla* – root; *satyera* – of truth; *sandhāna* – in search; *bhāgya-krame* – out of fortune; *yāra* – whose; *haya* – there is; *tāte* – in that; *avasthāna* – attainment; *se* – such person; *yāya* – goes; *vaikuṇṭha-loke* – in the spiritual planet called Vaikuṇṭha; *phire* – return; *nāhi* – not; *āse* – come; *e* – this; *vṛkṣera* – of tree; *mūla* – root; *yathā* – when; *se* – that; *puruṣa* – the Supreme Lord; *pāśe* – next to; *se* – such; *ādi* – primeval; *puruṣe* – in the Supreme Personality of Godhead; *adya* – seek; *kara* – do; *se* – that; *prapatti* – surrender; *janmādi* – creation and others; *se* – that; *yāhā* – whatever; *hate* – from; *prakṛti* – nature; *pravṛtti* – the beginning.

As men of lesser intellect can neither see the end
of endless skies above them nor from where the skies begin,
conditioned souls cannot conceive the true form of this tree,
condemning them to struggle in its grip perpetually.
The roots of this great tree cannot be cut by any force
and thousands of mistakes arise when fools attempt that course.
The single weapon of detachment only can succeed
in cutting down this strongly rooted worldly banyan tree.
On having cut this tree, the soul is fortunate and blessed
to search out and attain reality and truthfulness.

Such souls attain *Vaikuṇṭha* planets, never to return,
for God Himself is by this banyan's root, they come to learn.
And thus the wise surrender to the Lord who manifests
all things at any time that anything at all exists.

5) *nirabhimāna nirmoha saṅga-doṣe mukta* I
nityānitya buddhi yāra kāmanā nivṛtta II 14
sukha duḥkha dvandva mukta jaḍa mūḍha naya I
vidhijña puruṣa pāya se pada avyaya II 15

nirabhimāna – without false prestige; *nirmoha* – without illusion; *saṅga-doṣe* – in faults of association; *mukta* – liberated; *nityānitya* – eternal and temporary; *buddhi* – intelligence; *yāra* – whose; *kāmanā* – desire, lust; *nivṛtta* – disassociated, detached; *sukha* – happiness; *duḥkha* – distress; *dvandva* – duality; *mukta* – liberated; *jaḍa* – gross; *mūḍha* – foolish; *naya* – not; *vidhijña* – knowledgeable; *puruṣa* – the Supreme Personality of Godhead; *pāya* – attain; *se* – that; *pada* – situation; *avyaya* – eternal.

Released from false prestige, deceit, and bad association,
detached from lust, discerning fixed and changing situations,
the soul untouched by joy or sorrow leaves the worldly modes
and reaches, in surrender, the eternal Lord's abode.

6) *se ākāśe jyotirmaye sūrya vā śaśāṅka* I
āvaśyaka nāhi tathā kimbā se pāvaka II 16
sekhāne praveśa hale phire nāhi āse I
nitya-kāla mora dhāme se jana nivāse II 17

se – that; *ākāśe* – in the sky; *jyotirmaye* – illuminating; *sūrya* – sun; *vā* – or; *śaśāṅka* – moon; *āvaśyaka* – necessary; *nāhi* – not; *tathā* – there; *kimbā* – or; *se* – that; *pāvaka* – fire, electricity; *sekhāne* – there; *praveśa* – entry; *hale* – if happens; *phire* – return; *nāhi* – not; *āse* – come; *nitya-kāla* – forever; *mora* – My; *dhāme* – in planet; *se* – such; *jana* – person; *nivāse* – resides.

No sunshine is required to illuminate that place,
and nor is fire, voltage, or the moon in outer space.

My infinite abode is such that if one enters in,
one never wants to see a mundane residence again.

7) *yata jīva mora aṁśa nahe se apara* I
sanātana tāra sattā jīva-loke ghora II 18
ekhāne se mana āra indriya-bandhane I
karṣaṇa karaye kata prakṛtira sthāne II 19

yata – as many; *jīva* – living entities; *mora* – My; *aṁśa* – part and parcel; *nahe* – not; *se* – such beings; *apara* – of anyone else; *sanātana* – eternal; *tāra* – of such beings; *sattā* – nature; *jīva-loke* – in the world of conditioned life; *ghora* – dark; *ekhāne* – in this place; *se* – that; *mana* – mind; *āra* – and; *indriya* – senses; *bandhane* – in bondage; *karṣaṇa* – struggle; *karaye* – doing; *kata* – so much; *prakṛtira* – of material nature; *sthāne* – in place.

The numberless eternal souls are spirit sparks of Mine,
existing in this world where they are physically entwined.
Their restless minds and senses keep them tightly wrapped and bound
and struggling to find some joy where little can be found.

8) *bāra bāra kata deha se ye prāpta haya* I
eka deha chāḍe āra anye praveśaya II 20
vāyu gandha yathā yāya sthāna sthānāntare I
karma-phala sūkṣma sei deha dehāntare II 21

bāra – again; *bāra* – and again; *kata* – so many; *deha* – bodies; *se* – such living entity; *ye* – that; *prāpta* – attains; *haya* – there is; *eka* – one; *deha* – body; *chāḍe* – leaves; *āra* – and; *anye* – in another; *praveśaya* – enters; *vāyu* – air; *gandha* – fragrance; *yathā* – just like; *yāya* – moves; *sthāna* – one place; *sthānāntare* – to another place; *karma-phala* – fruits of activities; *sūkṣma* – subtle; *sei* – that only; *deha* – body; *dehāntare* – at end of body.

Accepting situations born from mother after mother,
the fallen souls seek pleasure in one body or another.

As wind moves many fragrances, the spirit soul collects
conceptions of enjoyment in this body and the next.

9) *śarīrera anusāra śravaṇa darśana* I
sparśana, rasana āra ghrāṇa vā manana II 22
se śarīre jīva kare viṣaya sevana I
baddha-jīva kare sei saṁsāra bhramaṇa II 23

śarīrera – of the body; *anusāra* – according to; *śravaṇa* – hearing; *darśana* – vision; *sparśana* – touch; *rasana* – taste; *āra* – and; *ghrāṇa* – smell; *vā* – or; *manana* – think; *se* – that; *śarīre* – in the body; *jīva* – living entity; *kare* – do; *viṣaya* – objects of senses; *sevana* – service; *baddha-jīva* – conditioned soul; *kare* – do; *sei* – that only; *saṁsāra* – world; *bhramaṇa* – moving around.

Enjoying mind and senses, with desires at the helm,
the soul proceeds to see and taste and touch and hear and smell.
Conditioned souls thus hanker for, according to their birth,
a set of sensate objects as they roam about the Earth.

10) *mūḍha-loka nā vicāre ki bhāve ki haya* I
utkrānti sthiti bhoga kāra vā kothāya II 24
yāra jñāna-cakṣu āche gurura kṛpāya I
bhāgyavāna sei jana dekhivāre pāya II 25

mūḍha-loka – foolish people; *nā* – not; *vicāre* – judge; *ki* – how; *bhāve* – in method; *ki* – what; *haya* – there is; *utkrānti* – quitting; *sthiti* – situation; *bhoga* – enjoyment; *kāra* – whose; *vā* – or; *kothāya* – where; *yāra* – whose; *jñāna-cakṣu* – eyes of knowledge; *āche* – available; *gurura* – of spiritual master; *kṛpāya* – by mercy; *bhāgyavāna* – fortunate; *sei* – such only; *jana* – person; *dekhivāre* – to see; *pāya* – able.

Repeated births and deaths are all these foolish souls attain.
Enchanted by their bodies, they see nothing more to gain.
But if one has a kindly guru, all of this can change,
for birth and death are evident to one whose eyes are trained.

11) *kata yogī vaijñānika ceṣṭā bahu kare* I
ātma-jñāna abhāvete vṛthā ghuri mare II 26
kintu yevā ātma-jñānī ātmāvasthita I
dekhite samartha haya śuddha avahita II 27

kata – so many; *yogī* – transcendentalists; *vaijñānika* – scientific; *ceṣṭā* – endeavor; *bahu* – many; *kare* – do; *ātma-jñāna* – knowledge of self-realization; *abhāvete* – due to non-availability; *vṛthā* – unnecessary; *ghuri* – encircle; *mare* – die; *kintu* – but; *yevā* – when; *ātma-jñānī* – one who is self-realized; *ātmāvasthita* – situated in the self; *dekhite* – to see; *samartha* – qualified; *haya* – is; *śuddha* – pure; *avahita* – awareness.

So many yogis use techniques that lack this point of view.
Rebirth and death encircle them, no matter what they do.
But those who are self-realized, whose consciousness is pure,
begin to see the soul as their enlightenment matures.

12) *ei ye sūryera teja akhila jagate* I
candrera kiraṇa kimbā āche bhāla-mate II 28
āmāra prabhāva sei ābhāsa se haya I
āmi yāke ālo di-i se ālo pāya II 29

ei – this; *ye* – that; *sūryera* – of the Sun; *teja* – splendor; *akhila* – whole; *jagate* – in the world; *candrera* – of the moon; *kiraṇa* – ray; *kimbā* – or; *āche* – situated; *bhāla-mate* –properly; *āmāra* – My; *prabhāva* – influence; *sei* – that only; *ābhāsa* – illuminated; *se* – that; *haya* – there is; *āmi* – I; *yāke* – whoever; *ālo* – enlightenment; *di-i* – provide; *se* – such being; *ālo* – enlightenment; *pāya* – receive.

The endless, brilliant sunshine that pervades the whole creation,
and all the splendid moonbeams that obscure the constellations,
can only give their light because of My authority.
The light of anyone enlightened also comes from Me.

13) *ei ye pṛthivī yathā vāyu-madhye bhāse* I
āmāra se śakti dhare savete praveśe II 30
āmi se auṣadhi yata poṣaṇa karite I
candra-rūpe raśmi-dāna kari se tāhāte II 31

ei – this; *ye* – that; *pṛthivī* – world; *yathā* – where; *vāyu* – air; *madhye* – within; *bhāse* – floats; *āmāra* – My; *se* – that; *śakti* – energy; *dhare* – holds; *savete* – in everything; *praveśe* – enters; *āmi* – I am; *se* – that; *auṣadhi* – herbs and vegetables; *yata* – as much; *poṣaṇa* – maintain; *karite* – to do; *candra* – moon; *rūpe* – in form; *raśmi* – ray of light; *dāna* – supply; *kari* – doing; *se* – that; *tāhāte* – in that.

This planet and its atmosphere remain afloat in space
due only to My energy and all-pervading grace.
Varieties of vegetables and herbs can all survive
because of shining moonlight that I steadily supply.

14) *āmi vaiśvānara hai deha-mātra vasi* I
prāṇāpāna vāyu-yoge bhakṣya dravya kaṣi II 32

āmi – I; *vaiśvānara* – My plenary portion as the digesting fire; *hai* – am; *deha-mātra* – the body only; *vasi* – situated; *prāṇāpāna* – the outgoing and the down-going energy; *vāyu-yoge* – due to interaction of air; *bhakṣya* – that which is eaten; *dravya* – foodstuff; *kaṣi* – digest.

As well, I am the life air as it enters and retreats,
enabling all beings to digest the food they eat.

15) *sabāra hṛdaye āmi, sanniviṣṭa antaryāmī,*
āmā hate smṛti jñāna mana I
āmi se jāgāi kāre, āmi se bhulāi tāre,
āmā hate haya apohana II 33
yata veda pṛthivīte, āmāra se tallāsete,
āmi hai saba veda-vedya I
āmi se vedānta-vit, āmi ye vedānta-kṛt,
vedāntera kathā śuna adya II 34

sabāra – of everybody; *hṛdaye* – in the heart; *āmi* – I am; *sanniviṣṭa* – situated; *antaryāmī* – Supersoul; *āmā* – Me; *hate* – from; *smṛti* – remembrance; *jñāna* – knowledge; *mana* – mind; *āmi* – I am; *se* – that; *jāgāi* – make aware; *kāre* – someone; *āmi* – I; *se* – that; *bhulāi* – make forgetful; *tāre* – such being; *āmā* – Me; *hate* – from; *haya* – there is; *apohana* – forgetfulness; *yata* – as many; *veda* – Veda; *pṛthivīte* – in the world; *āmāra* – My; *se* – that; *tallāsete* – in search; *āmi* – I; *hai* – am; *saba* – all; *veda-vedya* – the knowable from the Vedas; *āmi* – I am; *se* – that; *vedānta-vit* – the knower of the Vedānta; *āmi* – I am; *ye* – that; *vedānta-kṛt* – the compiler of the Vedānta; *vedāntera* – of Vedānta; *kathā* – subject; *śuna* – hear; *adya* – now.

Established deep in every heart,
as Supersoul I then impart
a person's knowledge and their memory.
I help a person recollect
or force a person to forget.
Forgetfulness itself has come from Me.
In this world, all the Vedic texts
direct the seeker to reflect
and gradually come to knowing Me.
Eventually I alone
by all the Vedas can be known,
for I compiled and know them. Listen, please.

16) *baddha mukta puruṣa se haya dvi-prakāra* I
dui nāme paricita se kṣara akṣara II 35
baddha jīva yata haya tāra kṣara nāma I
akṣara kūṭastha jīva nitya mukta-dhāma II 36

baddha – conditioned; *mukta* – liberated; *puruṣa* – living entities; *se* – such; *haya* – there is; *dvi-prakāra* – two types; *dui* – two; *nāme* – in names; *paricita* – known; *se* – such beings; *kṣara* – fallible; *akṣara* – infallible; *baddha* – conditioned; *jīva* – living entity; *yata* – as many; *haya* – there is; *tāra* – of such being; *kṣara* – fallible; *nāma* – called; *akṣara* – infallible; *kūṭastha* – in oneness; *jīva* – the living entity; *nitya* – always; *mukta-dhāma* – liberated abode.

Each living entity exists in one of two positions;
the free souls live in My abode, while others are conditioned.
The liberated souls possess infallibility,
while others remain fallible until they live with Me.

17) *tāhā hate ye uttama puruṣa pradhāna* I
īśvara se paramātmā thāke sarvasthāna II 37

tāhā – these two; *hate* – from; *ye* – that; *uttama* – Supreme; *puruṣa* – Personality; *pradhāna* – main; *īśvara* – controller; *se* – such; *paramātmā* – Supersoul; *thāke* – resides; *sarvasthāna* – every place.

Besides these two there is the Greatest Personality,
the Supersoul, controlling and pervading all that be.

18) *kṣara vā akṣara hate āmi se uttama* I
ataeva ghoṣita nāma puruṣottama II 38

kṣara – fallible; *vā* – or; *akṣara* – infallible; *hate* – from; *āmi* – I am; *se* – that; *uttama* – transcendental; *ataeva* – therefore; *ghoṣita* – declared; *nāma* – name; *puruṣottama* – Supreme Person.

Because I am that transcendental Personality,
infallible and fallible do not apply to Me.

19) *ye more bujhila śreṣṭha se puruṣottama* I
sakala sandeha chāḍi haila uttama II 39
se jānila sarva veda nirmala hṛdaya I
he bhārata! sarva-bhāve se more bhajaya II 40

ye – one who; *more* – about Me; *bujhila* – understands; *śreṣṭha* – Supreme; *se* – such; *puruṣottama* – the Supreme Personality of Godhead; *sakala* – every; *sandeha* – doubt; *chāḍi* – leaving; *haila* – to be; *uttama* – topmost; *se* – such person; *jānila* – knows; *sarva* – every; *veda* – Veda; *nirmala* – pure; *hṛdaya* – heart; *he* – O; *bhārata* – son of Bhārata; *sarva-bhāve* – in every way; *se* – such person; *more* – to Me; *bhajaya* – renders devotional service.

The one who understands Me as the Personal Supreme
is free of doubts and knows Me as the best of everything.
That person, having understood the Vedic paradigm,
will serve Me well, in heartfelt pure devotion, all the time.

20) *ei se śāstrera gūḍha marma kathā śuna* I
tumi se niṣpāpa hao śuddha tava mana II 41
ihā ye bujhila bhāgye hala buddhimāna I
he bhārata! kṛta-kṛya se hala mahāna II 42

ei – this; *se* – that; *śāstrera* – of the revealed scriptures; *gūḍha* – confidential; *marma* – deep meaning; *kathā* – topic; *śuna* – hear; *tumi* – you; *se* – that; *niṣpāpa* – devoid of sins; *hao* – be; *śuddha* – pure; *tava* – your; *mana* – mind; *ihā* – this; *ye* – whoever; *bujhila* – understands; *bhāgye* – in fortune; *hala* – to be; *buddhimāna* – intelligent, wise; *he* – O; *bhārata* – son of Bhārata; *kṛta-kṛya* – the most perfect in one's endeavors; *se* – such person; *hala* – to be; *mahāna* – perfect.

Please hear these deep and secret *śastric* topics and begin
to act with a fresh mind that's purified and freed of sin.
O son of Bhārat, one who knows these secrets, blessed and wise,
achieves perfection in pursuit of any enterprise.

bhaktivedānta kahe śrī-gītāra gān I *śune yadi śuddha bhakta kṛṣṇagata-prāṇa* II

bhaktivedānta – of His Divine Grace A. C. Bhaktivedānta Swāmi Prabhupāda; *kahe* – speaks; *śrī-gītār* – of Śrimad Bhagavad-Gītā; *gān* – song; *śune* – after hearing; *yadi* – if; *śuddha* – pure; *bhakta* – devotee; *kṛṣṇagata-prāṇa* – absorbed in Kṛṣṇa consciousness.

Bhaktivedānta Swāmi thus recites *śrī-gītār gān*
to please the pure devotees always rapt in Krishna's song.

iti śrī-gītār puruṣottama-yoga nāmaka pancadaśa adhyaya samāpta I iti – at last; *śrī-gītār* – of Śrimad Bhagavad Gītā; *puruṣottama-yoga* – The Yoga of the Supreme Person; *nāmaka* – named; *pancadaśa* – fifteenth; *adhyaya* – chapter; *samāpta* – ends.

Thus ends the fifteenth chapter of Śrimad Bhagavad-gītā *named* puruṣottama-yoga *or the yoga of the supreme person.*

About the Authors

In 1965, equipped only with four dollars and a few books, **Śrīla A. C. Bhaktivedanta Swami Prabhupāda** arrived alone in New York City and proceeded to ignite a worldwide bhakti-yoga phenomenon. Although the seventy-year old Swami had never been out of India before, before his passing in 1977 he circled the world fourteen times, published seventy books, and established one hundred and eight centers of ISKCON, the International Society for Krishna Consciousness. Through his vast knowledge and a lifetime of devotion, Śrīla Prabhupāda attracted spiritual seekers from all walks of life from countries all over the world to learn and apply to their lives the ancient and venerated traditions of bhakti-yoga.

Today ISKCON includes over eight hundred locally organized temples, schools, restaurants and farms throughout the world, all centered on the teachings of Śrīla Prabhupāda's *Bhagavad-gītā As It Is*. Hundreds of millions of this and other books by Śrīla Prabhupāda have been sold in approximately eighty languages.

Kalakaṇṭha dāsa began practicing bhakti-yoga under Śrīla Prabhupāda's guidance in 1972. Since then he has become an accomplished practitioner and teacher, sharing bhakti with thousands through widely appreciated lectures, seminars and books including *A God Who Dances, The Saint Within,* and several others. He specializes in translating Sanskrit and Bengali poetry for English speaking audiences and in establishing ISKCON ashrams (hostels) for young bhakti-yoga practitioners in North America.

Swarūpa Krishna dāsa has actively practiced bhakti-yoga since 1994. Since 2002 he has been a leading bhakti-yoga teacher in Kolkata. In addition to Śrīla Prabhupāda's Gītār Gān, he has translated Śrīla Bhaktivinoda Ṭhākura's *Śaraṇāgati* and *Harināma Cintāmaṇi, Bhakti Vrikṣa modules* (from English to Bengali), and numerous Bengali quotations by Śrīla Bhaktisiddhānta Sarasvatī Ṭhākura Prabhupāda. He helps design introductory bhakti-yoga courses for students of ISKCON's Māyāpur Institute.

Acknowledgments

Many thanks to Tulasī Priyā devī dāsī, Keshihanta dāsa, Sucitra devī dāsī and Madan Mohān Mohinī devī dāsī for their proofreading and editorial input.

Endnotes

I The famous monkey warrior of Lord Ramachandra.

II Lord Krishna, who is the master of the senses.

III Partha is a name of Arjuna meaning, "The son of Kunti (also known as Pṛthā.)"

IV Krishna, who has fine black hair.

V Krishna, who is the shelter of all people.

VI Krishna, who killed the Madhu demon.

VII Arjuna, descendant of king Bhārat. Krishna is reminding Arjuna not to shame his great heritage.

VIII A *kṣatriya* is a warrior or an administrative leader.

IX Another reference to Arjuna as the son of his great mother Kunti.

X Krishna, who is complete in all six opulences (wealth, beauty, strength, wisdom, fame, and renunciation).

XI Demigods such as Indra, Brahma, Siva, and many others who supervise the affairs of the universe are subordinate assistants to Krishna, the Supreme Personality of Godhead.

XII Krishna, who takes away one's material attachment.

XIII Krishna, who is the husband of Laxmi, the goddess of fortune.

XIV Krishna, best of the Vrishni dynasty.

XV Brahman is Krishna's all-pervading, formless spiritual presence.

XVI *Brahmacaris* are celibate students of spirituality.

XVII As described in the title of Chapter 2, *sāṅkhya* refers to descriptive knowledge of the soul and the body by analytical study.

XVIII A powerful, wicked tyrant of ancient times.

XIX Krishna, the killer of the Madhu demon, is being asked by Arjuna to slay the demon of doubt in his mind.

XX *Vaikuṇṭha* is the kingdom of God, freed (*vai*) from anxiety (*kuṇṭha*).

XXI Sri Hari, a name of Krishna meaning, "He who takes away one's attachments."

XXII Brahmā is the first demigod in the universe. He engineers the material creation under Krishna's directions.

XXIII The Bharatas are Arjuna's noble ancestors.

XXIV Ananta Śeṣa, the massive snake whose countless mouths are always glorifying Lord Vishnu.

XXV Arjuna, the conqueror of sleep.

XXVI *Japa* refers to the meditation technique of reciting the names of God on each bead in a string of 108. The recommended names of God (mantra) for the current materialistic age are,
Hare Krishna, Hare Krishna, Krishna Krishna, Hare Hare,
Hare Rama, Hare Rama, Rama Rama, Hare Hare.

XXVII 'Three worlds' refers to the Vedic literature's general groupings of higher, middle and lower planets.

XXVIII *Dharmas* refers to all actions in pursuit of spiritual realization.

XXIX *Samadhi* means unbroken concentration in perfect meditation.

XXX A *Vaishnava* is a devotee of Vishnu or Krishna.

XXXI The stage of self-realization beyond material anxieties.

XXXII *Sastric* refers to knowledge from *sastra*, the Vedic scriptures.

XXXIII *Mokṣā* means liberation from the cycle of birth and death.

XXXIV *Bhagavān* realization refers to knowing God as a person, the most complete understanding.

5/20/23

To Pooja,

May Lord Kṛṣṇa bless you with bhakti throughout your life.

Kalakantha
Das

Manufactured by Amazon.ca
Bolton, ON

33719891R00111